6 -

ESSAYS ON PLATO

EDWARD P. BUTLER

Phaidra Editions, New York City 2018

CONTENTS

Preface

The aim of these essays is to grasp Platonism as the living root of the Western philosophical tradition before that tradition became hegemonic through the monotheist capture of the Platonic 'One'. To grasp Plato's thought in this fashion, I believe, is also to find a way forward for philosophy through a *metaphysics beyond ontology*. The key term I utilize in this respect is 'henology', a modern coinage from Greek *hen*, 'one', which expresses—in contrast with the inquiry into *what there is* and *what it is for something to be*, known as 'ontology', from Greek *on*, 'being'—Platonism's central concern instead with a *philosophical arithmetic* of *units*, their internal conditions of integrity and their external combinatorial possibilities. Within henology, multiple ontologies are possible simultaneously, and *what is* is no longer prescriptive for *what might be*.

Why does recovering Plato's polytheism play such an important role in these essays? In part, it is simply that once we remove the reification of the 'One Itself' which was necessary in order to make it serve to represent the monotheist's God, and which made the discipline of henology virtually otiose, not only does the general field of units constitutive for Plato's theory of manifolds emerge, but the Gods themselves naturally present themselves as an important category of units for Plato and subsequent ancient Platonists. But there is more to it than this. Henological analysis of the Gods as unique individuals, as proper-named entities or 'whos' as opposed to essences or

1

'whats', reveals the primordiality of this mode of existence, and this in turn speaks to one of the most powerful motives for the reaction against metaphysics in contemporary philosophy, namely the idea that metaphysics can only proceed on the basis of reducing difference to sameness, and uniqueness to repeatable identity. But this is metaphysics as ontology, and moreover, after the monotheist capture of the Platonic 'One', hegemonic 'ontotheology'. Henology, by contrast, reveals the 'who' as the simplest mode of unity. From this mode of unity an unfolding of further modes of unity, a *procession of being*, can be traced. This sense of procession, insofar as it is ultimately henological rather than ontological, has no inherent reference to *numbers of units* and hence exercises no reductionism. It places no demand that the multitude we experience be seen as "really" fewer things or one thing, though it can, so to speak, host any number of such accounts, whether theological, scientific, ethical, or aesthetic.

The henological account of the procession of Being reaches its fullest articulation in the last Platonists of antiquity, Proclus and Damascius, who have been the primary focus of my work since my doctoral dissertation. But it has always been my conviction that the Platonic system as elaborated by these later thinkers was no arbitrary development, but rested securely on the foundation of Plato's own thought and that of his earliest successors at the Academy. Hence, in parallel with my further work on the so-called 'Neoplatonists' after defending my dissertation, I began to work on interpretations of Plato's own thought which were not 'Neoplatonic' projections onto Plato, but which sought to discover interpretations from which the course of later Platonic thought could be projected organically, as is the case for other disciplines in which a continuity of general goals and methods across their historical development is relatively uncontroversial.

These writings by no means represent the completion of my work on Plato, but rather a collection of key works allowing the reader to take stock of my position. Four of the essays were previously published in journals: "Plato's Gods and the Way of Ideas" in *Diotima* 39 (2011); "Animal and Paradigm in Plato" in *Epoché* 18.2 (2014); "Esoteric City: Theological Hermeneutics in Plato's *Republic*" in *Abraxas* 5 (2014); and "Polytheism and the *Euthyphro*" in *Walking the Worlds* 2.2. (2016). The short piece that opens this collection, "Polytheism and Metaphysics (I): Divine

2

Relation", appeared originally online, in my column *Noēseis* from Polytheist.com, in September 2014, while the piece that closes the book, "On the Gods and the Good", is the text of a talk I gave at the Polytheist Leadership Conference in July of that same year. The long essay "Toward a New Conception of Platonic Henology" appears for the first time here; it was written at intervals between 2008 and 2013. As the most ambitious discussion I have so far produced of henology purely from the standpoint of Plato's own thought, it informs all the other essays, though inasmuch as it has remained unpublished, they never explicitly reference it.

Polytheism and Metaphysics (I): Divine Relation*

To recognize how fundamental polytheism is to Plato's metaphysics, one need only reflect on the *Timaeus*, in which the cosmos itself comes to be from one God beholding another God. One must let go of the notion that the significance of this lies in these being some *particular* Gods; approaching the text in this way is a monotheistic hangover, and a deafness to metaphysics, but it's curable. Metaphysics is all about forms, and it has no force of its own but the unforced force of being itself. A formal structure or formula is active over however wide a field to which it can apply, that is, over however much it expresses formally. A form as such therefore is most potent when taken at its most universal or abstract, while in its specificities its activity is more localized. Hence in the truly cosmogonic application of the formula of Demiuge and Paradigm in the *Timaeus*, these are *any* two Gods in *any* conceivable relationship with one another, every relationship in any myth you can think of. *Every myth*, understood in this way, is cosmogonic. *Beholding* is to be taken as the universal relationship here because consciousness, awareness

---

* This essay originally appeared in my column *Noēseis* on Polytheist.com on 9/03/2014 (http://polytheist.com/noeseis/2014/09/03/polytheism-and-metaphysics-i-divine-relation/).

4

of appearing, can accompany any action whatsoever, and therefore it represents or formalizes any action.

Nor need the cosmogonic relation be a relation between just two Gods—a concreteē relationship involving any number has the same value. By 'concrete', I mean that a merely categorial relationship, class membership, won't do, except insofar as that intellective act by us is traced back to its conditions of possibility, which lie in concrete cognitive acts of the Gods themselves. Membership in a class such as the class of all Gods is not the same logically as, for example, *being an Olympian*, which is a concrete relationship among individual Gods, and thus ontologically prior to formal classes. A cosmogonic relation can also consist in one God relating to Him/Her/Eirself *as* Another. Monotheists have obviously taken advantage of this possibility in order to make use of Plato's *Timaeus*, though not without some discomfort, but polytheistic theologies have always been capable of this move as well.

In Egyptian theology, when Atum masturbates in the precosmic waters, there are immediately five, at least, who emerge from His solitary act: Atum, who has affirmed Himself in the chaos, Nūn, from which He distinguishes Himself; His children, Tefnut and Shu—ejaculate/cosmic substance and void/cosmic space; and Atum's hand, Iusāas or Nebet Hetepet ('Mistress of Offerings') or Hathor. In Heathen theology, Odin sacrifices Himself to Himself to receive the runes, that is, to render the cosmos intelligible. Atum and Odin both in some sense sacrifice an Eye: Odin sacrifices His eye to Mímir's Spring (cp. English *memory*), while Tefnut, known as Atum's 'eye', which is also His 'agency' (two senses of Egyptian *irt*), becomes alienated from Him in the Nūn, and returns to become the uraeus cobra on His forehead, symbol of all the forces that defend cosmic order. In this way, both Gods have made independent an element of Themselves, a 'vision' in which all beings, as a result, participate, a sight no longer subjective but objective or intersubjective.

The cases in which the cosmogonic relation is internal to a single divine individual are thus in some way those in which the focalization, or viewpoint quality, the subjectively oriented nature of the relation is emphasized. But this serves the purpose of *making the entire field of relations objective*. Hence the point of these myths is still the fundamentality of relation, even if it is a relationship between potencies in a single individual. Thus the cosmogonic relation is framed in the *Timaeus* as an *intersubjective* relation, and this is its primordial state, because the intersubjective relationship is the richest in content, and it is from the intersubjective relation that everything requisite to cosmogony can be inferred. This becomes especially apparent when in the *Phaedrus* Plato speaks of the divine *symposion*. The *symposion*, alongside its richly specific Bacchic associations, is also a formal structure, standing for any place where the Gods, in being together with one another, behold in each another all that truly is and all virtue, a vision which spills over to dazzle and inspire the souls of mortals.

Plato's Gods and the Way of Ideas*

ABSTRACT: The article defends a systematic and not merely allegorical function for Plato's Gods as the eternal substrate for the Ideas. The reminiscence of the virtues immanent to the particular deity in whose company they "followed" prior to birth sensitizes mortals to virtues present in other mortals. On this analysis, the separate Idea is primarily necessary for mortals in their effort to cultivate divine virtues in mundane life.

In a well-known reading of the *Symposium*, Gregory Vlastos sees in Diotima's account of the ascent from appreciating the beauty of an individual body to glimpsing the essence of beauty itself Plato's inability to perceive individuals as ends in themselves.[1] Individuals are loveable only because and insofar as they instantiate certain qualities, and it would be "idolatry" to love them for their own sakes. Vlastos' interpretation of Platonic erotics follows quite naturally from interpreting Platonic ontology as categorically subordinating individuals to the ideas,

---

* Originally published in *Diotima: Review of Philosophical Research* 39, 2011 (Hellenic Society for Philosophical Studies, Athens), pp. 73-87. The pagination from this publication appears in the text in brackets.
1 G. Vlastos, "The Individual as an Object of Love in Plato," in G. Vlastos, *Platonic Studies* (Princeton: Princeton University Press, 1973), pp. 3-34.

reducing the former to mere bundles of qualities. Accordingly, White criticizes Vlastos' reading in the context of questioning this general ontological presumption, at least as it applies to Plato's early and middle dialogues.[2] Nussbaum, in *The Fragility of Goodness*, sees the *Phaedrus* as a sort of palinode in relation to the *Symposium* in which love is of the individual *qua* individual. More recently, without specific reference to the debate concerning Plato's erotics, McCabe, in *Plato's Individuals*, has argued that individuation, rather than being or form, is primary for Plato, for whom "The problems of 'being' … are attached to whether, and how, we can determine that something is an [**74**] individual" (305).[3] No response to Vlastos' position has taken account, however, of the significance of a particular class of individuals playing an especially important role in the *Phaedrus*, namely Plato's Gods. Commentators such as Griswold have indeed taken account of the Gods inasmuch as they are responsible for certain human 'character types', but not with respect to just what sort of beings, and what sort of individuals, *they* are.[4] I believe that understanding the role the Gods play in Plato's erotics will enrich our understanding of the relationship between individuals and ideas in Plato's thought more generally.

To accord any systematic role to the Gods in Plato's philosophy raises the issue of the degree to which it is appropriate to take Plato's references to them seriously, rather than as allegorical references to ideal principles. Even commentators who have been interested in this aspect of the *Phaedrus* have generally been interested in its subjective dimension, in a putative Platonic 'mysticism'.[5] Of the Gods

---

2 F. C. White, "Love and the Individual in Plato's *Phaedrus*," *Classical Quarterly* 40 (1990), pp. 396-406; cf. F. C. White, "Plato's Middle Dialogues and the Independence of Particulars," *Philosophical Quarterly* 27 (1977), pp. 193-213. White argues that Plato affirms a "tripartite world" consisting of particulars, forms and individual qualities in the early and middle dialogues alike, coming to regard particulars as reducible to bundles of qualities only with the *Timaeus*, if at all.

3 M. M. McCabe. *Plato's Individuals* (Princeton: Princeton University Press, 1994).

4 C. L. Griswold, Jr. *Self-knowledge in Plato's Phaedrus* (New Haven: Yale University Press, 1986).

mentioned in Plato's works, only the demiurge of the *Timaeus* usually receives serious consideration from modern commentators *qua* God. One reason for this is surely because the demiurge of the *Timaeus* is more compatible with the creator God of the dominant monotheisms than the Gods of the *Phaedrus*, which features a pluralistic divine field and is concerned primarily with inspiration (in the broadest sense) rather than with creation. Depending upon one's sense of what theology *ought* to be, then, Plato's 'theology' may be sought preferentially in his account, e.g., of the idea of the Good, rather than where he speaks explicitly about Gods.

Nevertheless, there has been some tendency among recent scholarship to allow for the possibility that Plato and Aristotle may have taken the Olympian theology rather more seriously than is generally assumed, for example Richard Bodéüs in *Aristotle and the Theology of the Living Immortals*, which refers in its title to the description of a God given at *Phaedr.* 246d1-3: "an immortal living being, [75] having a soul and a body joined together for all time."[6] To the degree that Plato subscribed to traditional Hellenic theology, his 'theology' would be external to his metaphysics; Bodéüs sees just this sort of "dissociation of theology from metaphysics" in Aristotle. Moreover, Bodéüs compares the relationship between the Gods and the intelligible in Aristotle to "the theses of Plato's *Phaedrus* concerning extracelestial intelligible entities," which "suggest that the gods' relation to these reputedly divine intelligible beings is not one of ontological identity, but one involving the gods as knowers of those intelligible beings," (40). Bodéüs separates both Plato and Aristotle in this way from the tradition of what he terms "Western onto-theology". As Bodéüs remarks, the term *theologia*, as first attested in *Rep.* 379a, "ne désigne pas une science, mais le langage de ceux, poètes ou prosateurs, qui parlent des dieux" (Bodéüs 1992, 247 n. 10). Plato's relationship to 'theology' in this

---

5 See, e.g., K. R. Seeskin, "Platonism, Mysticism, and Madness," *Monist* 59 (1976), pp. 574-586.

6 R. Bodéüs, *Aristotle and the Theology of the Living Immortals*, trans. J. Garrett (Albany: SUNY Press, 2000); see also R. Bodéüs, "La philosophie et les dieux du *Phèdre*," in L. Rossetti (ed.), *Understanding the Phaedrus* (Sankt Augustin: Academia Verlag, 1992), pp. 246-8.

sense is more complicated than Aristotle's. In the *Republic*, Socrates demands that discourses concerning the Gods conform to certain *tupoi* concerning what a God really is (*tôi onti*) which will determine the limits within which a literal reading of the myths is acceptable.[7]

Taking Plato's Gods seriously as a class of beings, however, and not merely as allegorical decoration around the Ideas nor, e.g., as planets,[8] is not without certain important consequences for [76] Platonic ontology. I shall argue that joining the account in the *Phaedrus* to that in the *Symposium* suggests that the ideas emerge out of the relationship between humans and the Gods and remain, in certain respects, a dependent moment of that relationship. In the Gods, the ideas possess an eternal substrate, a substrate which is not contingent because the Gods exhibit such excellences essentially. In this respect, the Gods are to the ideas generally what, e.g., fire is to the idea of heat (*Phaed.* 105c).

This understanding of the nature of ideas could be seen as one way of coping with the *aporiai* arising from the attempt to conceive of the ideas in sovereign independence. Parmenides demonstrates to the young Socrates that the doctrine of the ideas suffers from a number of difficulties which arise from conceiving of the ideas as things separate in themselves. These difficulties center on the problem of the relations which would obtain between ideas and particulars and culminate in a picture

---

7 The literal reading being as much as children, who are at issue in the passage from the *Republic*, can reasonably be expected to grasp. That Plato is not averse to symbolic interpretations of myth is clear from the "etymological" section of the *Cratylus*—if we choose to regard that text as being in earnest. For notable recent efforts at taking the "etymologies" seriously, see D. Sedley, "The Etymologies in Plato's *Cratylus*," *Journal of Hellenic Studies* 118 (1998), pp. 140-154, and J. Bronkhorst, "Etymology and Magic: Yaska's *Nirukta*, Plato's *Cratylus*, and the Riddle of Semantic Etymologies," *Numen* 48 (2001), pp. 147-203.

8 See Bodéüs 1992, 247; if, according to *Phaedr.* 246c-d, we have never seen a God, then the Gods cannot be the planets, which are visible as such—the planets are categorically distinguished by Plato in this fashion from the Gods of the tradition inasmuch as the latter are invisible, manifesting themselves when they will (*Tim.* 40d-41a).

according to which if the ideas indeed exist, they are nevertheless quite unknowable. It would take a person of both natural talent and wide *experience* to disprove this, Parmenides asserts (*Parm.* 133b). By characterizing his candidate in such a way, Parmenides seems to intimate that the answer will require inquiries or information transcending the narrowly dialectical. The doctrine of the ideas is on no account to be abandoned while it awaits its adequate defender; nor are we to imagine that the inference of the unknowability of the ideas is correct simply because it will be so difficult to refute it. This cannot be the case, Parmenides assures us, for were it, it would also lead us to the inference that the Gods are not our masters nor have any knowledge of our affairs (134e). The present essay argues that Plato answers this objection through an account integrating the origin of the ideas and the way in which humans achieve consciousness of them into a narrative about the relationship between humans and the Gods which is, at the same time, rich in ethical significance.

I. The *Phaedrus*

Beauty, among the ideas, projects itself the furthest into mundane life. The likenesses here of justice and of temperance and the other ideas have no light of their own, Plato explains, and so only a few come, with difficulty, to perceive them through their images (*Phaedr.* 250b). But beauty, which illuminates the realm of the Gods, shines its light as well here among us **[77]** and is thus perceived immediately by the senses, especially by the sense of sight, and by everyone in one fashion or another. Beauty alone plays this role according to Plato (250d). What is beauty, in the last analysis? We read that the divine (*to theion*) is the beautiful, the wise, the good, and "all other such things" [*pan ho ti toiouton*] (246e). This makes it seem that divinity somehow *encompasses* if not all, then at any rate the noblest of the ideas. But it does not seem as though a merely conceptual analysis of divinity would yield these qualities. The identity of the divine with these qualities must be of a different order.

We see the way in which beauty in particular interacts with the peculiar attributes borne by various Gods in the account Plato offers of erotic attraction. Humans who find themselves on the Earth together at a given moment have been, prior to their return into bodies, followers or attendants of various deities. Socrates explicitly remarks that he was a follower of Zeus, and presumes this of Phaedrus as well (*Phaedr.* 250b). This prenatal cultic affiliation, so to speak, manifests itself in our patterns of erotic attraction. Plato goes into quite a bit of detail. The God to whom we are affiliated affects not only the qualities we find attractive in another, but also our style as lovers and the qualities which, once we have found a partner, we seek to bring out simultaneously in them and in ourselves. In loving our human lover, we honor and imitate the God or Goddess whom we love (252c-253c). The beauty of the God or Goddess impresses upon us as well a special receptivity to the virtues which that particular deity both embodies and inculcates. The beauty of the Gods is, so to speak, a delivery device for virtues. The virtues we honor are, therefore, present to us to begin with as an integral part of the individual nature of the deity to whom we are affiliated.

Indeed, Plato speaks of the ideas such as justice and temperance as "honored" (*timia*) by souls (250b2), and uses the same terminology to refer to the activity of "honoring" one's patron deity in the beloved (252e1). The term *timai* was, of course, in use at least since Hesiod to refer to the potencies, the particular spheres of influence, of the various Gods. Here we see that for Plato, the virtues are, from a point of view of their origin, certain potencies or attributes of the Gods. Mortals are sensitized to these potencies by the adoration they experienced before birth for the deity whom they "followed", and so they seek to bring these attributes out in themselves [78] and in their romantic partners. This desire drives them to learn the nature of the attribute (or attributes) from whoever they can, as well as to search within themselves for the traces of the nature of the God which are fixed in their memory (252e6-8). As Plato explains,

> when they search eagerly within themselves to
> find the nature of their God, they are
> successful, because they have been compelled
> to keep their eyes fixed upon the God, and as
> they reach and grasp him by memory they are
> inspired and receive from him character and
> habits, so far as it is possible for a man to

participate in the God (253a1-6; trans. Fowler, modified).

The recollection of the ideas is integrated here with the factors eliciting it in mundane life in a way that substantially supplements the account in the *Meno*, which simply states that "as all nature is akin, and the soul has learned all things,"—i.e., in the discarnate condition—"there is no reason why we should not, by remembering but one single thing—an act which men call learning—discover everything else, if we have courage and faint not in the search," (81d1-5; trans. Lamb). To the *Meno*'s account of the conditions of the possibility for recollection, the *Phaedrus* adds the motives and the mechanisms of that particular experience of recollection, namely the recollection of divine beauty, which has the potential to drive the whole process of recollecting any number of diverse ideas from beginning to end, though different individuals may pursue it to different lengths.

We are accustomed to think of the ideas as something separate from the Gods, and yet the account in the *Phaedrus* never explicitly indicates this. Rather, it indicates that the ideas—at least the ones of which it treats—are bound up intimately in the organic unity of each divine person. Hence it is beauty, which pertains more immediately to the utterly particular and unrepeatable than any other idea, which delivers the ideas to the lover, who separates it out at last because their prenatal affiliation to a particular deity has sensitized them to it. For such a lover, the distinction of the form from its sensible bearer is a way of drawing nearer to the form's original, divine bearer.

The ideas, as they appear in the account of the supracelestial place in the *Phaedrus*, are not so much distinct and separate forms but rather attributes of real being and properties of the [**79**] supracelestial "place" itself. It is the Gods who are the prominent individuals in this place; Plato says that the Gods at their banquet "behold the things beyond heaven" (247c3), that the region or place itself possesses truly existing essence or substance (247c8-d1). There is talk of the justice, temperance and knowledge to be beheld there (247d2-e4), as well as other, unspecified real beings (247e3) and truths (248c3). But Plato is as likely to refer to these as *food* for the Gods, as he is to refer to them as *spectacles* enjoyed by them (247e3-4, 247d2-3). And he seems to make the distinct essences of the ideas less important than their common orientation to real being: the knowledge beheld by the Gods, for instance, is "that which exists in the essence of real being" (247e1-2). Real being is the quality of the place, and it is the sense of place which dominates the passage. The knowledge in that place is surpassing knowledge because it is the knowledge that is *there*, and similarly for the justice, the temperance, and so forth.

What gives to this place such an aspect? Why should we imagine it to be other than that it is the place where the Gods hold their banquet? Plato cannot have meant any actual spatial "place", for Aristotle attests that for Plato there is no extracelestial body, and that the Ideas are "nowhere" (*Physics* 203a8-9). The "place" Plato speaks of in the *Phaedrus* is, rather, uniquely defined by the presence of the Gods. Similarly, why should we imagine that what nourishes the Gods at their banquet is something other than the society and fellowship existing among them, where jealousy is unknown (247a9) and every virtue is there to be seen *in one another*?[9] In the *Protagoras* (347c-e), Plato stresses that the symposium of the *kaloi kagathoi* requires no "extraneous voice" of flute or harp "but only the company contenting themselves with their own conversation"— and this would be true *a fortiori* regarding a gathering of the Gods, the supreme *kaloi kagathoi*.

The remark at 249c, which might be taken to imply the subordination of the Gods to the ideas, says only that those things which collectively constitute real being are those things with which [**80**] the God is engaged *qua* divine (*pros hoisper theos ón theios estin*).[10] The significance of the supracelestial place, what

---

9 Cf. the reference to the "spiritual sustenance ... deities bring to the feast" in the *Laws* (653d; trans. A. E. Taylor).

10 In contradistinction to, e.g., Rowe, who reads "those things his closeness to which gives a god his divinity." But note that the *pros hoisper* here corresponds neither to the causal dative of, e.g., *Phaedo* 100 e5-6 nor the *dia* + accusative of *Phaedo* 101a-b, which can be regarded as characteristic of the ways in which Plato expresses the causality of forms in the relationship of participation (on which see S. Yonezawa, "Are the Forms *Aitiai* in the *Phaedo*?" *Hermes* 119 (1991), pp. 37-42. The Neoplatonist Proclus, for his part, explicitly denies that the Gods participate anything (*In Tim.* I, 364 Diehl); we should not assume without

14

gives to it its special quality as a place, is that it is a gathering *together*, in common, of the Gods who are otherwise "attending each to his own duties" (247a7-8).[11] In this respect, one might compare the supracelestial *topos* of the *Phaedrus* to the "space" or "receptacle" of the *Timaeus*, inasmuch as the latter is the medium for the appearance of forms in sensibles while the former is the medium for the appearance of divine virtue at the "symposium" of the Gods.[12]

II. *The Symposium*

Having referred to the banquet of the Gods, it is appropriate to turn to the *Symposium*, to an account which, as both the subject matter and the motif of the banquet would lead us to expect, both parallels and elaborates upon that in the *Phaedrus*. In the *Symposium*, however, the viewpoint remains within the human domain; hence, instead of a discourse about the Gods by a philosopher, there is a discourse by a priestess about the intelligible qualities of the divine, the two discourses thus forming a kind of chiasm.[13] Diotima thus parallels in some respects Timaeus, who [81] delivers a speculative discourse about cosmogenesis while leaving to the poets the empirical accounts, as it were, of the activities of particular Gods. Both discourses,

---

good reason that Plato imagines the Gods as participants in any sense which would subordinate them.

11 Cf. Proclus, *Theol. Plat.* I, 107: through divine beauty "the Gods are united to and rejoice in each other, admire and are delighted in communicating with each other and in their satiety/complementarity [*plêrôsis*]."

12 Cf. Manuela Tecusan's discussion of the significance of the *symposion* for Plato, with special attention to the discussion of drinking parties in the *Laws*, in M. Tecusan, "*Logos Sympotikos*: Patterns of the Irrational in Philosophical Drinking: Plato Outside the *Symposium*," in Oswyn Murray (ed.) *Sympotica: A Symposium on the Symposion* (Oxford: Clarendon Press, 1990), pp. 238-260.

13 To be sure, Diotima's discourse is still semi-mythical, just as Socrates' discourse, although he modestly describes it as a "game" (*Phaedr.* 265d1) nevertheless embodies the principles of dialectic (265d2–266c1).

however, are framed by an explicit respect for such Gods, the individual objects of cult: Timaeus begins his discourse with an invocation (*Tim.* 27c), while Diotima is clearly one of those "priests and priestesses who have studied so as to be able to give a reasoned acount of their ministry," (*Meno* 81b; trans. Lamb).

In the *Phaedrus* beauty and love act as the triggers to elicit the recollection of a host of different ideas; in the *Symposium* the nature of love itself is analyzed. Love is explained by Diotima as an intermediate nature connecting humans to the Gods, a *daimón* conceived during the celebration among the Gods of the birth of Aphrodite (*Symp.* 203b ff.). Love is thus distinct from Aphrodite, but occasioned by her. Love is a manifestation of the intermediate nature of humans, neither divine nor utterly estranged from the divine, but desirous of the qualities possessed by the Gods which we are close enough to them, at certain times, to perceive. Philosophy is of a similar intermediate nature (204a8-b2), bearing the same relationship to the generic divine attribute of *wisdom* as love bears to the generic divine attribute of *beauty*.

Two of the three generic attributes of the Gods from the *Phaedrus*, namely the beautiful and the wise, have thus been seen to yield daimonic strivings peculiar to them. Is there such a striving corresponding to the third attribute, the Good? To the good which is beyond being and source of being and essence to beings (*Rep.* 509b5-9) must correspond the most elemental of strivings, the striving to exist. Hence for Neoplatonists the good becomes the principle of individuation *par excellence*, the *sóstikon hekastou*, that which "conserves and holds together the being of each several thing," (Proclus, *Elements of Theology*, prop. 13; trans. Dodds). In desiring the One or the Good, entities desire their individual integrity. The striving after the One is individuative, just as the striving after wisdom makes one a philosopher and the striving after beauty makes one a lover. The striving after the Good makes one whatever and whoever one is. The quality, therefore, which it is most natural to identify as that quality in the Gods denoted by the generic divine attribute *the good* (*to agathon*, *Phaedr.* 246e2) is the attribute of perfect, integral individuality. The individuality possessed by each God impresses [82] their attendant souls so indelibly that they seek its likeness throughout their embodied lives. They must seek it, however, through *qualities*, and in order to do so effectively, they must go at least some way along the philosopher's path by understanding something of the essence of those qualities.

The erotic lover is distinguished from the lovers of other things—money, athletics, even philosophy (*Symp.* 205c9-d8)—because it is erotic love or love of beauty which is *ontologically* fundamental, the other loves being derivative. It is the love of beauty which brings the idea to birth in us, born out of mortals' nostalgia for the society of their chosen deities. This means that when they fall in love, the object, it is true, is not *simply* the beloved. The essence of the erotic bond is for Plato a sort of procreation (206b7-8), because there is a third created in any erotic bond. This mediating term stands, in some respect, between the lovers; and yet it also engenders a reciprocity which is as novel in Plato's context for the heterosexual as for the homosexual couple (206c6-7). Love in the primary sense is of generating or begetting in or upon the beautiful (206e5) any of the manifold of ideas which we know from the *Phaedrus* to be carried within the image of beauty impressed upon mortals by the vision of the deity in whose company they traveled. This "begetting" is the joint work of the lovers of generating virtue in each other and in the society.

The martial valor of Ares, the royalty of Hera, the intelligence and leadership of Zeus, the inspiration of Apollo (Ares: *Phaedr.* 252c8; Hera: 253b1; Zeus: 252e1-6; Apollo: 253b3, 265b4), and other virtues corresponding to the other Gods are brought to birth among mortals, both in thought and in action, as a product of mortals' yearning for the virtues' original, divine bearers. Nor does each God represent but a single virtue; each one must rather exhibit a mixture of many virtues, just as would any virtuous human. Thus White remarks (White 1990, p. 402 & n. 21) in regard to *Phaedr.* 252c-d that the lover models himself on the God whose follower he is, "in all the latter's characteristics, not just those that distinguish him from the other gods," from which "it follows that he strives to imitate his god in point of those qualities shared by all the gods." At the same time that it implies the possibility of an account which would abstract from the distinguishing characteristics to speak only of the qualities shared in common by all deities, [**83**] divinity as such, it would also follow from this aspect of the *Phaedrus* account that the deity him/herself is not reducible to a single quality, and that the Gods, whatever else we might say about their place in Plato's thought, do not simply *stand for* the ideas.

Collecting the many sensible instances into one logos was the human side of recollection in the *Phaedrus* (249b8-9); the ascent of Diotima's ladder, which begins from the encounter with a beautiful body, an encounter which already engenders beautiful *logoi* (*Symp.* 210a9-b1), constitutes a *logos* of beauty itself through the vertical series of beauty's manifestations. This pursuit of the idea *as* idea is what distinguishes the *Symposium* from the *Phaedrus*. The lovers in the *Phaedrus* are indeed driven to learn as much as they can about the virtue they seek to cultivate in their beloved and in themselves (*Phaedr.* 252e), but the point of this is to get the cultivation right, that is, the process which is spoken of in the *Symposium* as an engendering of virtue in one another by lovers. This fostering of virtue in the *polis*, as eminent a goal as it is, is spoken of by Diotima as being itself "for the sake of" certain "rites and revelations" (*Symp.* 210a1-3) in which one participates by ascending the ladder until one reaches the "essence of beauty" (211d1) or "uniform [*monoeides*] divine beauty itself" (211e5).

But the breeding of virtue in the *polis* is by no means forgotten by Diotima: seeing the beautiful in that which one sees—that is, seeing the idea of the beautiful—ensures that one will breed, not phantoms, but true examples of virtue (212a4-6). This throws into question the notion that the breeding of virtue was only "for the sake of" the ascent up the ladder. But it becomes clearer when we read that by engendering true virtue and rearing it, a person becomes *theophilês*, beloved of the Gods (212a8). One has become generically pleasing to the Gods in the process of becoming pleasing to the *particular* God with whom one is enamored. The accounts in the *Symposium* and the *Phaedrus* thus complement each other: the ascent up the ladder to the pure idea was for the purpose of ensuring that the virtue propagated in the *polis* was genuine and not counterfeit, because it is the cultivation in the *polis* of the virtues embodied by one's patron deity that wins the love of that deity. Instead of the erotic cultivation of virtue in the *polis* being for the sake of the ascent up the ladder, according to this view it is for the sake of becoming beloved by the God, to which end the ascent up the [**84**] ladder is also subordinated.

18

Plato's lover does not, therefore, love the human beloved alone. But the primary mediating entity in the erotic encounter is not an idea, but the reminiscence of Gods who are themselves individuals and even, in some sense, personalities, though perhaps not so anthropomorphic as in Homer. The *Phaedrus* does, as well, speak of human lovers journeying on together indefinitely through the rounds of metempsychosis (256d9), and so human individuals, too, hold their own in the triangular relationship of humans, Gods and ideas. In this triangle, the idea is a measure deriving its value from its position in an economy of human and divine in which the human is not opposed to the divine as mortal to immortal, because all soul is immortal, but as forgetful to mindful or unstable to stable. The instability displayed by human souls has a benefit, however, insofar as it results in humans begetting virtue in society, which makes of them something more than mere spectators of their tutelary deities, allowing them to manifest something of the Gods' presence in their human lives.

Contra Martin Warner, therefore, the individual is loved "full-stop", if it is qualities that provoke the question.[14] Warner finds the difference between the Christian concept of love and Platonic *erós* in that the former is "essentially personal" whereas the ultimate object of the latter is "the abstract form of beauty". But this is wrong on both counts. First, because as L. A. Kosman points out, the 'agapic' or 'unconditional' love Nygren and others oppose to Platonic *erós* does not have the individual as its object either, except accidentally.[15] In fact, the object of "agapic" love is merely another universal, the *human* as such. Secondly, the abstract form, as I have argued, ought to be seen not as an end in itself so much as a *moment* in the begetting of virtue in our realm. Hence the persistence of the mundane being through time is assimilated by Diotima to the account of metaphorical procreation: the sort of creatures that we are must beget *ourselves* anew all the time to persist, and [**85**] thus we require the application of the paradigm if we are to grow

---

14 M. Warner, "Love, Self, and Plato's *Symposium*," *Philosophical Quarterly* 29 (1979), pp. 329-339.
15 L. A. Kosman, "Platonic Love," in W. H. Werkmeister (ed.) *Facets of Plato's Philosophy* (Amsterdam: Van Gorcum, 1976), pp. 56f.

into/beget our best possible self. There are more than two individuals involved in the bond of love; but the ontological framework of an economy of individuals is not compromised by the recourse to forms.

Conclusion

Do we love virtue because it reminds us of the Gods, or do we love the Gods because they manifest virtue? The preceding account has alerted us not to be too quick to hypostatize the ideas when the Gods are in the picture. The souls of mortals are unstable, and therefore the virtues are, and must be, conceivable as separate from them; and it is naturally accidental for forms to be instantiated or known in beings such as these. The Gods, by contrast, are not in the same predicament. They are immortal and so is their virtue and their knowledge; the virtues and the forms need no separate eternity, if to be a God is something more than merely to be immortal, but also implies immortality in the state Plato knows as "blessedness". As Socrates states in the *Republic*, "It is impossible for a God even to wish to alter himself; rather, it appears that each of them being the most beautiful and the best possible abides forever simply in his own shape," (*Rep.* 381c6-9); and for Aristotle (*Politics* 1323b23-26) the God is blessed "not because of any exoteric good but through himself, on account of being a nature of a certain kind," and the well-being of the Gods and the cosmos alike lies in that they "have no actions concerned with externals beyond the things proper to them," (1325b28-30).

The eternal perfection of the Gods is such that beauty and the rest are not in them as "somewhere" and "in something different" (*Symp.* 211a9). In this sense, it is for us that the ideas come into being *qua* "separate" ideas, because it is we who perceive them always with some constitutive non-identity, whether in recollection of our Gods, or as present in our beloved, perhaps unsteadily and yet compellingly, but always also "somewhere else". We love virtue because it reminds us of the Gods, but that does not mean that virtue is not loveable in itself; it is, but it requires an individual locus from which to shine forth. This position corresponds in certain respects to that of Eric Perl,[16] who argues for understanding the [86] transcendence of the forms in such a way that "while the forms cannot exist without instances, they are not therefore dependent on them" (351), and hence the transcendence of forms is compatible with their requiring a locus of some kind:

> [T]he insistence that in all periods of Plato's thought the forms are present in instances does not in any way compromise or diminish their transcendence … But this transcendence must not be conceived in dualistic terms … The fundamental point of Plato's theory, rather, is that transcendence is not elsewhere but in our very midst. (361)

Whereas Perl, however, finds the locus of the forms in sensible particulars—where indeed they *are*, insofar as it is constitutive for the form *qua* form to appear in sensibles from which it also separates itself as its "presentations" or "appearances"—the present essay finds their ultimate, eternal and necessary locus in the Gods. This position might seem to be in starkest contrast to the "extreme monadism" advanced by Mohr,[17] for whom the forms are "both fundamental individuals and fundamentally individuals" (115). The present essay agrees, however, with the latter characterization while disputing the former. That is, Mohr makes a strong case for the forms being fundamentally individuals but not for *which individuals they are*. And the characteristics which he attributes to "the Platonic 'to be'," viz. 'to be actual', 'to be substantial', 'to be there in such a way as to provide an object to point at', 'to present itself'," (125) are surely most appropriate to the Gods, to whom at any rate one cannot claim without argument that Plato would have *denied* this sense of "being" in favor of entities (the forms) whose ontological *status* he never really attempts to explicate.

---

16 E. Perl, "The Presence of the Paradigm: Immanence and Transcendence in Plato's Theory of Forms," *Review of Metaphysics* 53 (1999), pp. 339-362.

17 R. D. Mohr, "Forms as Individuals: Unity, Being and Cognition in Plato's Ideal Theory," *Illinois Classical Studies* 11 (1986), pp. 113-128.

Furthermore, we must recognize that Plato does not attempt a comprehensive catalog of the ideas or the virtues, nor should we thus assume a God is exhausted by one or two virtues abstracted from them. The nature of individuality is such that we can never exhaust an individual conceptually; instead we must, in the words of the *Philebus*, after discerning as many forms as we can within the unit we are analyzing, "let each one of all these intermediate forms pass away into the unlimited" (*Phil.* 16e; trans. Hackforth). [87] The limit of intelligible determination is the unique individual, and the richest sense of individuality, that is, personality, implies its expression in an inexhaustible dialogical intersubjectivity.[18] Griswold is correct to say that the *Phaedrus* indicates that "[t]o be a god is to live beyond the split beyond the subjective and the objective," but he is mistaken to construe this as "freedom from perspectivity" (Griswold, op cit., 109). There is also in intersubjectivity that which transcends the split between the subjective and the objective, but it lies not in simple identity, but in reciprocity. Is the "perfect objectivity" of "thought thinking the purely intelligible" only to be found in, e.g., the geometry of the *Meno*, or is it to be found as well, and even primarily, in divine intersubjectivity? The separation between the intelligible object—the "nourishment"—and its contingent instantiation would belong, then, to *our* mode of being, which is why *we* need to abstract the forms as measures. Failing to accord the proper status to the Gods as individuals makes it likely we shall undervalue human individuals, misidentifying that which is mortal, so to speak, in the mortal individual as the latter's "perspectival" mode of being (104-5 & 266 n. 46), as if because we are individuals "the preservation of our humanity is not wholly desirable" (106). On the other hand, one might find the value of humanity to lie in the degree to which it *formally underdetermines*[19] the individuality of beings in whom the transcendent ideas *show* themselves.

---

18 Cf. D. Nikulin, *On Dialogue* (Lanham: Lexington Books, 2006).
19 *Protagoras* 320d ff.; *Timaeus* 90e ff.

Animal and Paradigm in Plato*

ABSTRACT: The paradigm according to which the cosmos is ordered by the demiurge is characterized in the *Timaeus* as 'Animal Itself', while παράδειγμα in the vision of Er from the *Republic* denotes the patterns of lives chosen by individual humans and other animals. The essay seeks to grasp the animality of the paradigm, as well as the paradigmatic nature of animality, by means of the homology discernible between these usages. This inquiry affirms the value within a Platonic doctrine of principles of persons over reified forms, of modes of unity over substantial natures, and of agency over structure.

This essay concerns animals, including humans *qua* animals, insofar as they may be considered the *fundamental units* of the Platonic cosmos. The animal as considered in this fashion, however, is prior to taxonomy, and as such expresses a metaphysical 'humanity' prior to the taxonomically human; so this essay also concerns the animal *qua* human. The critical concept Plato provides us for grasping his thought in this way is that of the παράδειγμα, 'paradigm' or 'pattern', as it is used on the one hand in the vision of Er that concludes the *Republic*, and on the other, in the account of the demiurgic organization of the

* This essay originally appeared in *Epoché: A Journal for the History of Philosophy*, Vol. 18, Issue 2 (Spring 2014), pp. 311-323. The pagination from this publication appears in brackets.

cosmos in the *Timaeus*. We shall see that the term παράδειγμα is to be distinguished in important respects from other terms Plato uses for principles of formation, chiefly εἶδος, 'idea' or 'form', although the present essay can only begin to adumbrate the relationship between these terms.

In the vision of Er (*Rep.* 614b-621d), souls preparing for rebirth are presented with an array of possible paradigms for lives they might live. The possible lives include those of all kinds of animals as well as all sorts of human lives, and the choosers include those who have just completed human lives as well as those who have been animals. Humans may choose lives as humans again or as other sorts of animals, animals may choose lives as other sorts of animals, and animals may even choose human lives as well. We need not assume that Plato intends us to [312] take this account literally in every respect, but certain things follow if we take it seriously at all—and it is clear enough from the references to metempsychosis in other dialogues,[20] differing in some particulars but not very much, that Plato means us to make *something* of it, and something more than what would answer solely to the thematic needs of the *Republic*.

---

20 E.g., *Phaedo* 70c-72a, 81d-82b, 107d-108c, 113a; *Meno* 81b-c; *Phaedrus* 245c-257a; *Timaeus* 42b-d, 90e-91c; *Laws* 903d. I do not address in the present essay divergent aspects of these accounts, such as the judgment, not present in Er's vision, but prominent in the *Phaedo*, and mentioned elsewhere, e.g. in the *Apology* (41a) and *Gorgias* (523a-527a), where metempsychosis is not, or the possibility of release from metempsychosis in the *Phaedo*. There is, as well, Diotima's characterization of immortality as consisting for the individual either in procreation or the propagation of virtue (*Symp.* 207d-208e). Diotima's speech addresses a different problem, as I have discussed in "Plato's Gods and the Way of Ideas," *Diotima*, 39, 2011, pp. 73-87. The *Timaeus* account features below; I address briefly below a possible understanding of the release from transmigration. In general, I think the vision of Er may be regarded as normative in certain respects and with an eye toward certain problems, while other of these accounts might be regarded as normative in their own right and within the scope of the problems addressed in their particular dialogues.

One must acknowledge, first, that Plato wishes us, for whatever purposes, to at least imagine an extraordinary kind of existential choice laid upon the individual, a choice, moreover, that he wishes us to think of as free—"the cause [or 'blame', αἰτία] is his who chooses" (617e)—despite the virtually complete determination of the choice by the circumstances of the previous life, and the prior state of the cosmos in general. Second, one must acknowledge that he wishes us to imagine the individual who would make such a choice as somehow numerically the same across every conceivable qualitative variation, and thus to imagine a source of identity that goes to the very limits of what is conceivable as determinate identity, and perhaps beyond, since no quality exists by which we might identify an individual as the same over such a transformation, except for one alone. Only the agency exhibited in the existential choice itself can be regarded as the ultimate individuator of ensouled entities. If 'this soul' can be now a human, now a swan, now something else altogether, its identity can only be fixed, either by the series of forms itself in its utter contingency, or by the ideal unity of the one choosing each successive form. The 'freedom' of this choice, therefore, *purely with respect to its individuating character*, is presupposed by Plato, a presupposition perhaps rendered innocent just by virtue of the uncertainty of the individual's successful *appropriation* of the choice to him/herself. This imperfect identification with the agent of the choice corresponds to the sense of individuation in Plato as an "achievement", as it has been presented recently, e.g., by Mary Margaret McCabe and by Lloyd Gerson. For just as "being a unified person is not something I can take for granted … but rather something to which I aspire,"[21] being *the one who chose* in any sense beyond the emptily formal is not simply given to me.

Far from discouraging us from drawing ontological inferences from the account of the choice of paradigms in the *Republic*, the posteriority of the soul's order or structure (τάξις) to the choice itself—"But the τάξις of the soul was not there [among the paradigms], because from the choice of a different life inevitably a different <τάξις> comes to be" (618b)—

---

21 M. M. McCabe, *Plato's Individuals*, Princeton, Princeton University Press, 1994, p. 264. Cf. Lloyd P. Gerson, *Knowing Persons: A Study in Plato*, Oxford, Oxford University Press, 2003.

positively invites it, especially in light of Plato's assertion at *Philebus* 30b that both mind and soul come from the "family of cause [τὸ τῆς αἰτίας γένος] in all things." This cause or agency may "most justly be called wisdom and intelligence," but Plato does not quite assert their identity; as for soul, it is clearly treated as posterior to the family of cause, which "gives" (παρέχον) it to us. The temptation to read this as a reference to a single cosmic cause granting souls ought to be resisted. The purpose in this passage is to outline a *class* of entities to complement the classes of limit (limiting, measuring [**313**] and informing entities), unlimited (entities receptive of limiting, especially continua of whatever kind), and the mixed (entities conceived as a state of limit imposed upon some unlimited by a cause) in a classificatory system. A reference to a numerically singular cause of everything is, at least, not *required* in a discussion ostensibly concerning the *class* of causes, and hence the status of *causality* as such.

Fortunately, the individual agency displayed in the constitution of the soul provides an attractive alternative. Nor should it concern us if the single genus of 'cause' encompasses both personal agency and natural causality. While Plato divides causes into two classes in the *Timaeus* (46de), namely, the causes belonging to the intelligent (ἔμφρων) nature and those which "are of the class of things which are moved by others, and themselves, in turn, move others because they cannot help it," he is prepared elsewhere, in another light, to see this difference as one of degree, rather than of kind, as in the *Phaedo* (105ce), where soul is considered as a form-bringer of Life just as fire is a form-bringer of the Hot. The class of 'cause' in the *Philebus* in this way is free to exhibit as much diversity as the classes of limit, unlimited, and the mixed, and we can assume that in many cases a single entity would be, from different perspectives, cause, limit, unlimited, and mixture.

Indeed, the method of classification into causes, limits, unlimiteds, and mixtures would seem to be useful in the way the *Philebus* intends only insofar as the same entity can be regarded from different perspectives as belonging to different classes; for example, something that is in some respect a cause is in another respect a mixture, and so forth. This seems to be the case with the soul, considered now as a pure agency, now as the structure resulting from the operation of such agency. We are reminded of the formulations from the vision of Er when the *Philebus* states that "in the nature [φύσις] of Zeus ... a kingly soul and a kingly mind appeared through the power of the cause, and in other deities other noble qualities from which they derive their favourite epithets" (30d, trans. Fowler, slightly modified). Φύσις is used, e.g., at *Rep.* 620c, as a synonym for that which elsewhere in Er's account is more often termed βίος, a life or way of life, namely that structure which, through the choice of a paradigm, the individual brings forth. This structure expresses the different result that follows from one individual choosing a particular paradigm rather than another individual choosing the same one: same paradigm, different life. There could be little purpose, however, to individuating the paradigm in this fashion except as an ideal immanent to an already constituted βίος, or, better, a βίος in process of constituting itself. The paradigm appears in this light as a dependent and inseparable moment of the life, a moment problematic in its very nature. The 'idea' of the soul referred to at *Phaedrus* 246a is another way of referring to the structure resulting from the agency of the choice, which helps to clarify the young Socrates' ambivalence at *Parm.* 130c about whether there is an idea/form (εἶδος) of the human, or of fire, fire sharing the soul's status as a typical form-*bringer* in the final argument of the *Phaedo*. The ambivalence arises with [314] respect to attributing *form* to the causality of the form-bringer, and identifying the structuring agency with the resulting structure. Even if the form-bringer has a formal structure, is it structured *qua* cause, or *qua* effect of some other causality, and hence as a mixture in the *Philebus* classification?

The structuring cause in question then is not some single architectonic cause of the whole cosmos. Rather, each existing individual's agency is an orientation of desire which causes the individual to come-to-be in the form answering to it, a form proleptically, if also problematically, contained in the pattern or paradigm that is the actual object of the mortal soul's choice. A cause bringing about a life is distinguished from other causes in operating according to a paradigm, for here this agency can be most clearly distinguished from the structure or form, as is the case in animals, humans and Gods particularly, as opposed to form-bringers such as fire.[22] In such cases it is appropriate to

---

22 We may understand the notion of a final release from metempsychosis (see above, n. 1) in light of this theoretical

speak of a paradigm. This is essential to Platonic 'animality', as we shall see from considering the paradigmatic function of the 'Living Thing Itself' or 'Animal Itself', αὐτοζῷον, in the *Timaeus* in the direct relationship I believe it to bear to the paradigms implicated in the life cycle of each individual animal, whether human or other. 'Animal Itself', explicitly and repeatedly designated a παράδειγμα, and according to which the demiurgic God organizes the cosmic φύσις or nature, is itself paradigmatic of the paradigms chosen by mortal souls; it is the Animal as such, which means nothing more, and nothing less, than that each paradigm of a life, a βίος, is really *some animal.*

We ought to think of the relationship between the cosmic paradigm and the paradigms that embody the life-choices of individual animals as such that the cosmos acquires its organization not from a top-down determination, but from the bottom up through the very choices of souls, and its form is that of just such living, desiring intentions: an animal composed of animals. The very nature of a paradigm, I would argue, calls for this sort of conception. The cosmic paradigm, in this sense, *is* the paradigms of lives, and it is a transposition of registers to make it *another one* (cf. *Parm.* 132d-133a). Plato in this way grants epistemic authority to the animal's perspective on the world, according to the principle that "like knows like" (*De An.* 404b16). Moreover, it is the autonomy of these individual minds that enables the Gods to achieve the "easy supervision of all things" that the Athenian stranger describes in the *Laws* (903d-905c), in which the trend of our desires and the resulting state of our soul causes us to assume a position in the cosmos that secures the victory of goodness in the All by congregating like souls together so that the effectiveness of the better-intentioned souls is maximized, that of the worse-intentioned minimized. Similarly, at *Theaet.* 176e-177a Socrates speaks of παραδείγματα of "divine happiness" and "godless misery" in the nature of things; in doing injustice, one grows more like the latter and less like the former, the penalty for evildoers being simply living the

---

opposition between structure and structuring agency, namely, as securing the possibility *in thought* of a clean separation between these aspects of the individual. This possibility having been secured, it is no longer material whether such a separation really occurs.

life answering to the pattern they resemble, "in the society of things as evil as themselves." Accordingly, in the [315] *Timaeus* the forms, εἴδη, within the cosmic paradigm are not, e.g., discrete species, but instead *habitats*—astral, aerial, aquatic, and terrestrial (*Tim.* 39e-40a).

To come to be according to a paradigm seems to signify primarily that something is a *structured totality*. The aspect of totality is emphasized by Plato when he explains that the relationship of likeness (ὁμοιότης) between the cosmos and the paradigm does not consist in the privilege accorded some partial form (ἐν μέρους εἴδει, *Tim.* 30c). And so, in the first place, there is not some *particular* animal paradigmatic for the cosmos—for instance, the human. The universal 'humanity' which lies prior to the differentiation, first into genders, and then into other species of animal (*Tim.* 90e-92c) cannot be identified with the *particularistic* humanity which lies at the end of this process of speciation. I have spoken of this distinction between a wider and a narrower 'humanity' in another context.[23] As a result, the souls of humans and other animals do not differ in kind, for which Aristotle indeed seems to criticize Platonists (*De An.* 402b3-5). Carpenter has argued correctly, I believe, against the interpretation that would first generate 'prototype' animals from the primordially 'human' paradigm, with animals subsequently generating their own kind from these prototypes without reference to their original 'humanity'.[24] Rejecting such prototypes means that the injunction from *Phaedrus* 249b, that only a soul that has beheld truth may enter human form, lays no categorical restriction upon the passage from the animal to the human form, for every soul is primordially 'human' in the special, paradigmatic sense.

Viveiros de Castro has found a very similar structure in Amerindian, especially Amazonian, mythical ontologies, for which "the original common condition of both humans and

---

23 "Hercules of the Surface: Deleuzean Humanism and Deep Ecology," in B. Herzogenrath (ed.), *An (Un)Likely Alliance: Thinking Environment(s) with Deleuze/Guattari*, Newcastle upon Tyne, Cambridge Scholars Publishing, 2008, pp. 139-158.

24 A. D. Carpenter, "Embodying Intelligence: Animals and Us in Plato's *Timaeus*," in J. Dillon and M. Zovko (eds.), *Platonism and Forms of Intelligence*, Berlin, Verlag, 2008, pp. 39-57; p. 48 & n. 24.

animals is not animality but, rather, humanity," such that the task of the myths is to tell "how animals lost the qualities inherited or retained by humans [...] Animals are ex-humans (rather than humans, ex-animals)." These ontologies exhibit a concept of humanity with a broad and deep metaphysical significance transcending taxonomic determination; 'humankind' in this sense is "the substance of the primordial plenum or the original form of virtually everything, not just animals."[25] This notion of humanity finds a direct expression in language, in a phenomenon which has been mistaken, Viveiros de Castro argues, for mere 'ethnocentrism':

> [T]he Amerindian words which are usually translated as 'human being' and which figure in those supposedly ethnocentric self-designations do not denote humanity as a natural species. They refer rather to the social condition of personhood, and they function (pragmatically when not syntactically) less as nouns than as pronouns. They indicate the position of the subject; they are enunciative markers, not names [...] Thus self-references such as 'people' mean 'person', not 'member of the human species', and they are personal pronouns registering the point of view of the subject talking, not proper names. To say, then, that animals and spirits are people is to say that they are persons, and to [**316**] attribute to non-humans the capacities of conscious intentionality and agency which define the position of the subject.[26]

---

25 E. Viveiros de Castro, "Exchanging Perspectives: The Transformation of Objects into Subjects in Amerindian Ontologies," *Common Knowledge*, 10.3, 2004, pp. 463-484; p. 464-5.
26 Idem, "Cosmological Deixis and Amerindian Perspectivism," *Journal of the Royal Anthropological Institute*, 4.3, 1998, pp. 469-488; p. 476.

To be 'human' is, in effect, to occupy the first-person position of cause and of agency, rather than the third-person taxonomical position of the mixture, to return to the categories from the *Philebus*. In the same way, Viveiros de Castro finds complementary and opposed to the category of the 'human' in this first-person, subjective sense the objectivizing ethnonym applied to the other: "Ethnonyms are names of third parties; they belong to the category of '*they*' not to the category of '*we*'."[27] The ethnonym therefore stands in the place of the taxonomic distinction as such, whether applied to the other *or* when applied by the subject to him/herself *qua* object.

Thus there is a far-reaching metaphysical significance to the generation of humans and other animals *individually* rather than according to types. For the universal 'humanity' that is the starting-point for the emergence of every kind of animal, as well as the differences of gender and of every conceivable way of life as well, does not merely stand outside of, but *resists* speciation and sortal individuation. It is from the paradigm's *totality* that Plato infers the *uniqueness* of the cosmos (*Tim.* 31a). Rather than reducing individual animals to their part-status, the relationship to the paradigm, that is, the relationship of each animal to *its own* paradigm, gives form, not to a species, but to an *individual life*, and in this way affirms the uniqueness that is constitutive of a living thing as such. 'Humanity' thus is the intelligible expression of the metaphysically fundamental mode of unity, the mode of the *autos*, the 'self' as such, that is, as *each* self, not some single over-self. As Viveiros de Castro puts it with respect to the Amerindian ontologies, "the subjective aspect of being"—i.e., 'humanity' as the transhuman 'I'—is "the universal, unconditioned given [...] Reflexive selfhood [...] is the potential common ground of being."[28] Humanity in this special sense is thus *metaphysical individuality*.

This uniqueness of the animal inheres in its pure unitary agency, not in the animal as this or that *type* of mind or soul—or, *a fortiori*, this or that type of body (cf. Viveiros de Castro's remarks on the 'performative' nature of embodiment in the Amerindian ontologies).[29] Mind and soul as *products* can be

---

27 Idem, "Cosmological Deixis and Amerindian Perspectivism," *loc. cit.*, p. 476.
28 Idem, "Exchanging Perspectives," *loc. cit.*, p. 466-7.

regarded as homoiomerous substances on the analogy of elements like fire (*Phil.* 29b-30b), just as the latter can be regarded as an agent 'form-bringer' producing warmth. These two possible perspectives upon the living being are expressed in the paradigm itself. 'Animal Itself' is the animal of which all other animals are parts (μόρια), both individually (καθ'ἕν) and according to kind (κατὰ γένη) (*Tim.* 30c). Yet, it is not *as parts* that animals are 'paradigmatic', but as each a *whole* (ὅλος), i.e., an organism, and even, in a certain respect, each as the *totality*, as the All (πᾶν). From a henological perspective, that is, with respect to the inquiry into *modes of unity and of individuation*, what is important about the cosmic individual is the [**317**] convergence in it of internal or absolute individuation—that is, individuation by virtue of internal unity and coherence—and external or contextual individuation—individuation by virtue of exhaustion of some continuum specific to a given unit.[30]

In contrast to the paradigm, what we might term the partial form, that is, the species form, on the other hand, is treated by Plato as the repository of restrictive habits that inherently distort the possibilities of the cosmic individual. This is obvious in the shocking account in the *Timaeus* (90e-92c) of the generation of females and diverse types of animals from character flaws occurring through the declension, so to speak, of the universal 'human', an account, however, which resembles in broad terms the Amerindian mythic ontologies of how animals 'lost' their humanity—or how 'humans' lost their ability to participate in the wider, trans-species humanity. Proclus points out in his commentary on the *Republic* that the vision of Er shows that, in the absence of philosophy, all human perfections (such as the ways of life ranked at *Phaedrus* 248d2-e4) can be regarded as, in effect, so many modes of animality (*In Remp.* II 319.12-320.4 Kroll), that is, taxonomic animality. In Proclus' reading, virtues, even traits apparently divine (δοκοῦντα δαιμόνια), and not merely flaws, generate animal bodies in the presence of passion and without philosophy (316.6-25). Agamemnon, an embodiment of kingly virtue, admirable for his patience and perseverance (*Crat.* 395a), and whom Socrates looks forward to meeting in the

---

29 Idem, "Cosmological Deixis and Amerindian Perspectivism," *loc. cit.*, pp. 478-82.
30 M. M. McCabe, *Plato's Individuals, loc. cit.*, pp. 163-170.

afterlife (*Apol.* 41b), chooses a life as an eagle (*Rep.* 620b); Orpheus, a transmitter of divine inspiration (*Ion* 536b), chooses a life as a swan, even as a swan chooses the life of a human (*Rep.* 620a). What is distinctive about such 'animalities' is the manner in which they position the individual as part of a mediated whole (an ecosystem, a society) by emphasizing some part of the self (a particular talent, a peculiar antipathy) at the expense of its own totality, which reflects *immediately* the totality of the cosmic individual.

Only philosophy, which orients itself *away* from the human in the particularistic taxonomic sense—the objectively human, as it were—preserves the cosmogonic value of the individual. This value accrues, not to the animal as part of a species, even the human species, albeit that species has clear advantages in its ability to understand and appropriate for itself the paradigm. Cosmogonic value applies, instead, to the animal as a unique, and hence *totalizing*, individual. The individual is totalizing in its uniqueness inasmuch as this very uniqueness identifies it immediately with the totality of the cosmos, whereas a species, partial role, or specializing function of any kind represent mediations of this identification, these latter all being relationships of *whole and part*. To be some species of animal is no different than to have any of the other sorts of life experiences that predispose the souls in Er's vision to choose one sort of paradigm or another. These utterly unique life-experiences, and the unique trajectories they impose [**318**] upon souls, play a structuring role in the cosmos metaphysically *prior* to elemental forces operating with uniform regularity.

Appropriating a paradigm represents accepting a place, a part, in the cosmic whole constituted by the totality of the paradigms available to souls to select at any given moment. How such idiosyncratic paradigms—a paradigm, for example, of "a female artisan" or of "a private man who minds his own business" (*Rep.* 620c)—could possibly be conceived separately from the individuals who live them out, as well as the manner of whole formed by such parts, is obscure. The mechanism of the numbers drawn by the souls to determine the order in which they shall make their selection (617e) evokes the element of non-identity in this most individuating choice. Balancing the alienating aspect of the numerical lot is the assurance that "even for him who comes forward last, if he make his choice wisely and live intensely [σύντονῶς], there is reserved an acceptable life,"— ἀγαπητός, which can be read as 'cherished', or more often with the sense 'good enough'; for typical Platonic usages compare *Phil.* 61e, *Laws* 918e—"no evil one" (619b; trans. mod.). But since the field of patterns among which souls may choose is common for all, every creature depends, in some respect, for the kind of soul it shall come to be, upon the choices made by every other with whom its life shall overlap on the earth. The totality generative of souls is thus not a transcendent model generating copies, but an *immanent* totality, a virtual cosmopolis, participation in which forms the ultimate citizenship. Thus Socrates anticipates the unique paradigm of the individual when he speaks of a παράδειγμα of the city "of one's own" that may well not be "the city of one's birth", but which is "laid up in heaven for him who wishes to contemplate it and so beholding to constitute himself its citizen. But it makes no difference whether it exists now or ever will come into being. The politics of this city only will be his and of none other" (*Rep.* 592ab, trans. Shorey).

The ultimate role accorded to philosophy in the *Republic*, as supplied by the vision of Er, is to aid the individual in the utterly private and idiosyncratic act of personal demiurgy. In this respect, the account emphasizes the failure of souls to examine sufficiently the patterns they choose. Thus the soul drawing the first lot in Er's vision "at once sprang to seize the greatest tyranny [...] in his folly and greed [...] and failed to observe that it involved the fate of eating his own children, and other horrors" (619c, trans. Shorey). This Thyestes had lived in a well-ordered polity in his previous life, but having participated in virtue merely by habit—i.e., as a part, an organ, so to speak, of the state—and not through philosophical insight, he had no resources with which to choose wisely, or at any rate, none with which to choose *autonomously*. "One may perhaps say that a majority of those who were thus caught were of the company that had come from heaven, inasmuch as they were unexercised in suffering" (619d)—in a dialogue which has dwelt at such length on the forms of polity, here is a reminder that the purpose of that discussion [**319**] was to facilitate the soul's self-understanding. But beyond this, let us note that Plato offers here a means of dramatically leveling the playing-field between humans and other animals, for *suffering*, which would have helped

34

such a soul to choose well even without philosophical insight, knows no species. Setting aside for the moment the admittedly very small numbers of souls to be reckoned as philosophers, there is a broad common way for souls that embodies the justice of the whole cosmic order, and a common way of individuation as well.

Similarly, when Plato recounts that "… of the other beasts some entered into men and into one another, the unjust [ἄδικα] into fierce creatures, the just [δίκαια] transformed into gentle, and there was every kind of mixture and combination" (620d; trans. mod.), we may well be surprised to see 'justice' and 'injustice' unhesitatingly applied to nonhumans. This must be a justice that arises, not from rational insight, but from a well-ordered soul, in a manner that presents a continuum between the animal and the human state. A well-ordered animal soul will tend to seek, according to this account, more peaceful forms. But every form is useful to the "easy supervision" of the universe evoked in the passage cited above from the *Laws*. Specifically, animal forms in Er's vision serve to transmute passions into virtues. Ajax, nursing his grievance over the arms of Achilles, chooses the life of a lion, spurning the human form (620b). Plato obviously comments here upon the fit of insane rage in which, in Sophocles' tragedy, Ajax slaughters sheep and cattle, thinking them the Greek leaders who have disgraced him. A hero become ignoble in the throes of passion becomes here a creature who kills dispassionately to survive. Ajax can more easily manifest virtue as a lion than as a human who would begin from the place where the son of Telamon ended; he can be a just lion who could no longer be a just human.

In choosing paradigms for their lives, animals, including humans, choose a direction or orientation to which the cosmos adjusts, so to speak. In this process, the role of philosophy is to advocate for a greater degree of insight into, and hence control over, the processes that will shape the new person. This process is 'humanization' in the true sense, the sense which is not bound to the human species for any reason beyond the possibilities this form offers for the individual to grasp this process and therefore to manifest autonomy. Indeed, in accord with the aims and methods of Platonic henology, it ought to be possible ultimately to render the differences between one type of soul organization (τάξις) and another purely as a question of modes of unity, i.e., of

σύνταξις (*Rep.* 462c), and the 'human' defined in this fashion rather than according to purely contingent attributes (e.g., 'featherless biped') *or even essential ones* (e.g., 'rational animal'). The paradigm serves a cosmogonic function broader than the aims of philosophy; broader, as well, than the concept of a pattern or plan in the conventional sense, which points to a broader sense of *formation* in Plato than the stereotype of transcendent forms.[31]
[320]

If we look to the ways in which Plato uses the term παράδειγμα, we find that it rarely has the straightforward sense of an intelligible formative principle. Rather, it usually means an *example*, and this often in an ambiguous way. First, there are, of course, both good and bad examples, not just in social life (many of the uses of παράδειγμα as 'example' come from the sphere of crime and punishment), but also in epistemic inquiry. At *Theaet.* 202e, Socrates explains that we may hold as 'hostages' for a theory the examples (παραδείγματα) in terms of which it has been stated, for a theory may be undermined by the examples used to articulate it. This is in accord with the method for the use of examples explained in the *Statesman*, in which "an example is formed when that which is the same in some second, unconnected thing is rightly conceived and compared with the first, so that the two together form one true opinion" (278c, trans. Fowler, slightly mod.). A paradigm comes about from comparison, but the 'rightness' of this comparison can always be questioned; and, as the *Theaetetus* passage affirms, paradigms are not just used to articulate a theory, they are also crucially involved in theory formation. The ambiguity of paradigms lies in their dual nature as both coming prior to, and coming after, a process of formation. This underscores something else important about the term: more than any other term Plato uses for formative principles, 'paradigms' are themselves clearly and unmistakably particulars, as we can see from the discussion of forms as παραδείγματα in the *Parmenides* (132d), which occasions the famous 'third man' problem. Another important aspect of the paradigm can be see from *Rep.* 472bc, where the purpose of a παράδειγμα is to permit approximation, as opposed to the

---

31 For further considerations regarding 'forms' as such in Plato, with special reference to the *Phaedrus* and *Symposium*, see my "Plato's Gods and the Way of Ideas."

realization of an ideal. Just as in the *Parmenides*, the relationship constitutive of the paradigm is *likeness* (ὁμοιότης), not *sameness* (ταὐτότης), the relationship of likeness being analyzed, in effect, in the *Statesman* passage as that which is "the same in the different" (ταὐτὸν ἐν ἑτέρῳ). A paradigm has in this respect a certain priority to being itself, for "Do you think [...] that he would be any the less a good painter, who, after portraying a pattern [παράδειγμα] of the ideally beautiful man [...] should not be able to prove that it is actually possible for such a man to exist?" (472d, trans. Shorey).[32]

The paradigm in Plato and elsewhere has recently been the subject of a wide-ranging but incisive essay by Giorgio Agamben. Agamben does not discuss the use of παραδείγματα in Er's account or in the *Timaeus*, but his conclusions about the epistemological function of the paradigm as such are in harmony with those of the present essay. Agamben emphasizes the singularity and immanence of the paradigm, which "neutraliz[es] the dichotomy between the general and the particular [...] In the paradigm, there is no origin or *archē*; every phenomenon is the origin, every image archaic."[33] Agamben argues that there is a paradigmatic procedure in dialectics which embodies the latter's transcendence of the procedures of the special sciences, as treated in *Rep.* 509d-511e. In the special sciences, certain hypotheses are treated as principles, ἀρχαί, while in dialectics, hypotheses [**321**] are treated purely as hypotheses, in order to arrive at a non-hypothetical principle; for Agamben, inasmuch as "the knowability of the paradigm is never presupposed [...] treating hypotheses as hypotheses means treating them as paradigms" for this is to consider the ἀρχή "in the medium of its intelligibility."[34] The *idea* as such arises from and is dependent upon this procedure, "not another being that is presupposed by the sensible or coincides with it," but "the sensible considered as

---

32 Compare Proclus, for whom *likeness* is at once posterior to formal identity, as approximation-to-form, but also *prior* to form, inasmuch as likeness is the basis of all ontic procession (e.g., *Elements of Theology* prop. 29).

33 G. Agamben, "What is a Paradigm?", in *The Signature of All Things: On Method*, trans. L. D'Isanto with K. Attell, New York, Zone Books, 2009, pp. 9-32; p. 31.

34 Idem, "What is a Paradigm?", *loc. cit.*, p. 25 sq.

a paradigm."[35] The present essay argues to the same end by asserting the primacy of structuring causes to reified structure in Platonic ontology.

How, then, is the paradigm in the epistemological sense related to the paradigm of a life and the cosmic paradigm? What is the common structure, the paradigm of paradigms? The Eleatic Stranger speaks of the need for an example of how examples work at *Statesman* 277d, but is there a paradigm encompassing the epistemological as well as the zoogonic senses of παράδειγμα? If there is, it seems as though it would lie in the essentially *problematic* nature of both. That is, a paradigm, whether existential or epistemic, has the character of a problem, in the sense in which Proclus speaks of 'problems' as the analogues of production in theoretical sciences (*In Eucl.* 77 Friedlein/63 Morrow), "propositions whose aim is to produce, bring into view, or construct what in a sense does not exist" (201/157). The theorem is privileged over the problem within a discipline such as geometry, but geometry is a certain "dream about being" (*Rep.* 533c). The privilege of the theorematic over the problematic within such a special science cannot thus be regarded as a general ontological proposition once the broad scope of paradigmatic production in the *Timaeus* is taken into account, because the *Timaeus* takes up the question of the construction of the cosmos itself and everything in it. So too, the "city in speech" of the *Republic* is not an idea or form (εἶδος), but a παράδειγμα (*Rep.* 472e). It will not suffice to convert the ultimate paradigm into another dogmatic 'dream'.

What is paradigmatic about the paradigm is nothing other than its *animality*. What is essential to animality, as the vision of Er affirms, is desire, and the cosmic paradigm is the ultimate *object* of desire. But if it is the *ultimate* object, then it cannot be an object in this sense, but must rather be that which makes the desired object in its objectivity desirable (epistemologically speaking, "the medium of its intelligibility"); and this is simply the desiring itself as the primary mode of causality, cause of the organism.[36] In this way, we are thrown back again and again

---

35 Idem, "What is a Paradigm?", *loc. cit.*, p. 26.
36 Compare Theophrastus' critique of Aristotle's prime unmoved mover at *Metaphysics* 5b7-10, to the effect that circular motion is not the best motion if it is done for the sake of some

upon the individual desiring animal(s) as the sole intelligible content of the cosmos. For in what lies the "self-identical" nature of the paradigm, which ensures the beauty of the work executed in orientation toward it (*Tim.* 28a)? What paradigm could possibly be *unique* (31a)? The answer to these questions ought not lie in a violent transcendence. The animal is self-identical because it is, by definition, that which strives to persist in self-identity, and this striving is the beauty of every work the living performs. The paradigm is unique inasmuch as it [**322**] is each unique being *qua* unique, and uniqueness is nothing other than absolute individuation, dependent upon no sortal unit; and this is the animal as such, as structuring rather than structure. The demiurgic production of the cosmic totality is thus integrated into a broader framework of *action* and of ethical rather than technical formation (cf. *Nic. Eth.* 1140b6-7).

---

external object of desire, because *any* such motion will therefore be inferior to the motion providing the faculty of desire itself.

Esoteric City: Theological Hermeneutics in Plato's Republic*

> The other is speaking . . . of happy banqueters
> at a festival but not in a state, rather, he would
> be speaking of something other than a state.
> — Plato, *Republic* 421a–b[37]

> The souls arriving all the time . . . departed
> gladly to the meadow and encamped there as
> at a festival.
>
> — *Republic* 614e

When Plato's *Republic* criticises the poets and the "imitative" arts, it begins with the critique of *mythic* poetry and derives its impetus from it, and so to understand the significance of this critique we must grasp the significance of myth itself. If we make this effort, we shall find that myth, in its relationship to the Gods and to mortals, is at the very heart of the *Republic*'s metaphysical

---

* This essay was originally published in *Abraxas: International Journal of Esoteric Studies* 5 (2014), pp. 95-104. The pagination from this publication appears in brackets.
37 Translations from the *Republic* (*Politeia*) are generally those of Paul Shorey (Cambridge, MA: Harvard University Press, 1937), though I have often modified them.

concerns. Myth's value is not for entertainment or edification, but for salvation: "And so, Glaucon, a myth was saved and not lost, and it will save us if we believe it" (*Republic* 621b). But how do we believe? And how are we thus saved?

Myth is a revelation that connects us to the Gods, but any connection also separates the things it connects. In particular, a literal reading of myths may lead us to a conception of the Gods inconsistent with the mode of being properly divine. We need an "esoteric" reading of myth that looks to "underlying meanings", *hyponoia*. Representation, in turn, cannot be the sole or highest function of the arts, if it is the presence of the *symbol* that makes the arts divine. The imaginal City of the *Republic* is itself a symbol for the work of art, and the strictures applied to its citizens have at their heart the canons applied to myths, just as the Gods' cults lie at the centre of the City's public life. And the life of citizens beyond the City's walls, in the *festal* community of the city first described by Socrates and derided as a "city of pigs" – evoked again in the dialogue's closing eschatological myth of Er, as seen in the quotations above – is a symbol of the Gods' existence beyond the confines of narrative. The activity of esoteric interpretation, in restoring our recognition of the Gods' integrity, thus symbolises the restoration of our own integrity, while to become a citizen of the esoteric City is to enter the work of art.[38]

The *Republic* is a key classical locus for the very notion of esoteric interpretation, on account of its explicit reference to *hyponoiai*, "underlying meanings", possessed by the myths. The later Platonic tradition took up this practice, and so for instance in Proclus's commentary on the *Republic* we see the method applied to the mythic incidents Socrates refers to in the dialogue. Proclus explains that "symbols [*symbola*] are not imitations of those things of which they are symbols," and thus "If a poet is inspired and manifests by means of symbols" – literally

---

38 In the Platonic interpretation of the *Iliad*, the city of Ilios is the material (*hylikos*) site where the struggle over the status of embodied beauty is staged, and in this respect Homer's epic already suggests a symbolic identification of the City with the work of art. See "A Theological Exegesis of the *Iliad*, Book One", in my *Essays on a Polytheistic Philosophy of Religion* (New York: Phaidra Editions, 2012).

"tokens", *synthêmata*, a technical term in theurgy – "the truth concerning beings, or if, using science, he reveals to us the very order of realities, this poet is neither an imitator, nor can be refuted by the arguments [in the [**96**] text]."[39] So the mythic poet has access to a *science*; if we accept Proclus's argument that rescues the divinely inspired artist from mere representation, can we take the further step of determining a role for this science within the *Republic*'s concerns?

Esotericism of the City: The City as *Synthêma*

This question concerns, in the first place, the symbolic value of the *Republic* itself. The *Republic* discusses the constitution of a city as an analogy of the soul, for Socrates proposes to analyse justice in the soul through an enquiry into justice in a city. The *symbolic* value for the soul of the "city in words", however, is a different matter from the city as *analogy* of the soul.

In Plato's account, it becomes clear that souls and cities mutually condition one another to the point that statecraft is as much the art of forming souls, and of forming *a soul*, as of forming a state, these activities being inseparable. Beyond this, the soul is a citizen in the cosmos – even the souls of other animals, which are also, like us, part of the cosmic animal discussed in the *Timaeus*, the dialogue following on the *Republic*'s heels. For what is an animal composed of animals (*Timaeus* 30c–d) but a polity? Such a "state" can hardly, however, be assimilated without remainder to the political state, and indeed, there are likely to be points at which these "states" come into conflict.[40] Justice, as the discussion develops, turns out to be virtually synonymous with temperance (*sôphrosunê*). That is, justice is a harmony of faculties in the soul and in the state, not

---

39 *In Remp.* I 198.15–16, 20–4 Kroll.

40 Aristotle, in his *Politics*, recognises that the unity of the *polis* described in the *Republic* is such that it is no longer a city at all, but an individual (1261a15–24). Rather than taking Aristotle's criticism as destructive, I would argue that we may treat it as elucidating the very manner in which we ought to conceive the *Republic*'s city (cf. my remarks about the nature of *paradeigmata* in "Animal and Paradigm in Plato", *Epoché: A Journal for the History of Philosophy* 18.2 (2014).

in isolation, but in their intimate linkage. Justice is the harmony of souls in the state and in the state of the soul, the harmony between the faculties or powers within it which come into expression and sometimes conflict as an animal develops. Temperance is the virtue of understanding the proportions proper to a unity born of and borne by mixture, and so evidently requires the "Promethean" method taught in Plato's *Philebus*, the art of understanding all beings as mixtures, or as we might say today, as *structures*. But units are mixtures insofar as they are *caused*, while insofar as they are *causes* themselves they have a different status.[41]

Citizens, too, therefore, are never *only* citizens, parts of the more or less healthy organism that is their city or state, even if they are scarcely conceivable in isolation from such wholes. Moreover, the citizen-soul as part of the polity's mixture is inseparable from the mixture within the soul, from the soul itself as mixture. Plato elaborates a sophisticated psychopolitics in which different kinds of states arise from and foster certain states of the soul. Each type of soul and state has a particular relationship between whole and parts – a tyrant or a tyranny, an oligarch or an oligarchy, a democrat or a democracy – and there is no priority between state and soul in these fusions. It is not a matter of the state as a snapshot of its citizens' souls at any given moment, or of the soul's order being simply imposed by its environment. Rather, citizens' souls are always being shaped by the dispositions of power within their city and the city is always being transformed by the conflicts within the psyches of its inhabitants. Nor are either of these states ever really stable, but are always in some process of transformation, as well as being subject to forces from outside. The organism is always in an environment, always defines itself relative to some exterior. Even the cosmic animal, which is [97] unique in relation to its paradigm (*Timaeus* 31a–b) and exhausts the matter available to it (32c–33a), has externalities beyond it, relativising it, as recognised and articulated by later Platonists.

---

41 The Promethean method: *Philebus* 16c–17a; the addition of the notion of cause to the method: 26e–27c. I discuss the opposition of structuring causality and reified structure in Plato's thought further in "Animal and Paradigm in Plato".

To grasp this exterior, we need to begin from the city that is sketched by Socrates at the beginning of the dialogue and lies conceptually outside the City whose constitution he goes on to frame. Plato's brother Glaucon unsympathetically brands it a "city of pigs" (372d) due to the simple, though happy, lifestyle of its citizens. Responding to Glaucon's demand to frame a polity that can produce luxuries for an elite, Socrates begins anew, fashioning a city that can survive under conditions he describes straightforwardly as unhealthy, indeed "fevered" (372e). This city will accordingly belong no longer to pigs, but rather to hounds and sheep (422d). The sheep include both the producers and the leisure class for whom Glaucon was so keen to provide, while the hounds are the "guardians" (*phylakes*) whose asceticism, together with the producers' labour, makes the elite's indulgence possible. Eventually, however, the discussion purges from the city its unproductive elite (399e), despite the fact that all the strictures of the guardians were conceived on their account. This dialectical performance can only be seen as first positing, then negating a certain teleology, or even as expressing the limits of teleology as such. The desire for a surplus beyond the basic needs of life has proven to be a heuristic mirage. The ideal city has transcended the illusions that conditioned its emergence. It has come into its own as a self-sustaining organism, not eternal, like the cosmic animal, however, but flourishing for a time before declining into the senescence of oligarchy.

Behind and within this political account, which is already stipulated to be also and even primarily a psychogony, there is a hidden infrastructure of theology and soteriology to be unearthed. Plato tips his hand at one point (469a) with respect to his guardians, who turn out to be none other than the guardian *daimones* of Hesiod's Golden Age, "by the plans of great Zeus . . . guardians of mortal human beings" (*Works and Days* 122f). And these *daimones* are, in turn, clearly none other than those whom each soul, whether human or another animal, chooses when they select a "paradigm" or pattern of life (617d), according to the *Republic*'s closing discourse of Er, who died and returned to life. Between the account of the interval between lives and the account of the idealised state there are manifold parallels, and hence many threads available that can lead one safely through Plato's labyrinth. Another example is the "lots" (*klêrous*) that determine the order in which souls will choose their life-patterns, just like the lots governing the marriages of the guardians in the city (617d; 460a). These threads can, if pulled, loosen some of the knots that form in Plato's account if taken incorrectly.

Hence, it becomes clear that democracy is ontologically basic among the different state forms, despite representing a decline from the city of guardians, for in the democratic state, in any event, "one is not at a loss for paradigms [*paradeigmata*]" (557d–e), and the democratic soul "contain[s] within himself the greatest number of paradigms" (561e). The democratic state, therefore, for all its shortcomings, expresses most transparently the "meadow" in which the souls of all animals choose their life-patterns and form a lifetime bond, a marriage of sorts, with the [98] *daimón* who shall be "the guardian of his life and the fulfiller of his choice" (620e). The soul in the meadow and the citizen in the democracy share the common task of framing for themselves an imaginal citizenship in a polity in words, a city that is a "paradigm laid up in heaven" (592a–b).

Esotericism in the City: Exegesis and the Soul

Within Plato's construct of the most fully ordered condition of the state and/or the soul, since it is a portrait, at least from a certain perspective – portraits always being perspectival (598a–b) – of the cosmos as a whole, we can expect to find the Gods. Already in the "city of pigs", people "sing hymns to the Gods" (372b), and the city of guardians, likewise, should "admit no poetry . . . save only hymns to the Gods and the praises of good men" (607a).

Socrates considers the *logoi* concerning the Gods – the elements, as it were, of theology – through promulgating certain critical "guidelines" (*typoi*) for compositions involving the Gods. These canons can be reduced to the single maxim expressed at 381c, that "each God is the most beautiful and the best thing possible". This maxim, a key early statement of the doctrine I have characterised as polycentric polytheism, is at odds with a central characteristic of narrative, and of the state as well. In this context it is indeed perhaps important to speak of the state, rather than the city, because these do have a divergent trajectory in the history of thought. Whereas the city lets its wholeness be conceived as nowhere other than in each singular perspective on it, and invites therefore a polycentric conception, the state aims at the monocentric codification of sovereignty. This ambivalence has its ontologically primary expression, I would argue, in the problem of narratives about the Gods. We see this in particular at 379c–380c, where it is affirmed that in the guardians' city, speakers and poets will have to affirm that the Gods are not causes of *all things*, but only of *goods*. As a result, the Gods will actually have to be regarded as the cause of *few* things. This reasoning, however, which infers directly from the idea of the Good to the activities of the Gods, would strike at the heart of the Socratic project, enunciated in the *Phaedo* (97c ff.), to understand *all* things according to the Good.

There is a clash here, apparently, between a wide and a narrow conception of the Good, and corresponding to it a wide and narrow conception of the Gods' causality. According to the wide view, the Gods must be regarded as the cause of all things, and all things therefore as somehow of the good or from the good, while according to the narrow view, subsidiary causes must be assigned to those things that are not unequivocally good. Narrow goodness renders mythic narrative both necessary and problematic. The world's complex causality requires the conflict of diverse goodnesses: myth supplies this in conflicts among Gods, heroes and mortals, but also already in the notion of a division of labour among the Gods. The mythic narrative is thus theologically problematic in that it tends to make the Gods appear limited, partial and passive. But this is the very problem of the City of the Gods, of the sovereignty exercised by one such as Zeus in a heavenly state such as Olympos. Olympos is not a place, but a regime. Zeus's problem is to establish a division of labour, of "honors", *timai*, a term used persistently in Hesiod's *Theogony* and echoed by Plato when speaking of the articulated [99] functions within the state (for instance, at 434a). The Gods in mythic narrative, like the citizens in the state, cede their autarchy, and in a sense therefore their individual integrity, to a common whole, a common work (though humans, unlike the Gods, do so primarily out of need, out of an impossibility of autarchy for them (369b)). Mortal souls recover their integrity, such as it is, on the festal meadow upon which they must choose their *paradeigmata*, their life-patterns. Only by briefly recovering in the meadow their individual wholeness can souls, in a moment as free as they can experience, express what they truly find beautiful, what they truly want.

The Gods, on the other hand, recover their wholeness or autarchy from within the problematic justice of the narrative "state" through the art of *esoteric exegesis*. In the city of guardians as framed by Socrates, the place of exegete is held by Delphic Apollo, "who, seated at the centre and upon the navel of the earth, delivers his interpretation" (427c). As regards "the institution of temples and rites and other cultus of the Gods, daimons and heroes," which are "the greatest, the most beautiful and the first of institutions," of these there is no science, but they will come from the Gods themselves, and will thus be internal to pantheons: "if we are wise we shall … make use of no other exegete than our hereditary [God]" (427b–c). We learn from Plato's *Laws* that "hereditary" has no distinctly genealogical force here, for there the colonists founding a new city in a land already inhabited are urged to preserve the cults instituted by the natives, and "render them the same honours as did the ancients" (*Laws* 848d), alongside the Olympian cults the colonists have introduced, though these ancient cults are in no literal sense "ancestral" for the colonists.[42] What matters is the role accorded to institution (*nomothesis*) as complementary to science (*epistêmê*).

There is accordingly an ambiguity regarding exegesis, which is on the one hand internal to a tradition, but also belongs to philosophy, which bridges traditions. In the *Laws*, all references to "exegetes" posit their activities as internal to the Hellenic theology (759c, 775a, 828b). In the *Republic* passage, Apollo's role as exegete is "hereditary" for Hellenes, but Socrates also says that Apollo is "for all humanity the interpreter of [their] hereditary [religion]" (427c). Plato is hardly ignorant that other nations have their own theologies and exegetical practices internal to them. Rather, he seems to assert a special role for Apollo here as a patron of *philosophy*, though not in the same sense as Zeus, the patron of the philosopher in the *Phaedrus* (252e–253a). Among the abundant references to Apollo in Plato's works, most telling perhaps is the etymology offered for his name in the *Cratylus* (404e–406a), where Apollo is at once the one causing a manifold to "move together" (*homopolôn*) in harmony, and the one who is "simple" (*haplous*), that is, rather than complex or heterogeneous. The relationship between

---

42 Translations from the *Laws* are by R. G. Bury (Cambridge, MA: Harvard University Press, 1926), sometimes modified.

harmony in a manifold and the integrity of a unit, whether the city-state or the individual soul, is the very theme of the *Republic*. A God like Apollo has a role internal to his pantheon and also a role mediating between that tradition and certain universal – i.e., emptily formal – epistemic practices; and we can expect that Gods with similar patterns of activity in other pantheons will play similar roles empowering the 'translational' practices of philosophy or equivalent discourses.

Esoteric exegesis falls under this second of the exegete's roles, that which has to do not with [100] instituting cults and rituals, but rather with a kind of critique. The esoteric interpretation of myth is a critique of mythic narrative on behalf of the integrity of each God in the polycentric manifold; its goal is to recover the sense of each deity as the wider good.[43] The goal of such exegesis is not rationalistic "demythologization", because myth is cosmogonic. In the *Republic*, the cosmos is the "state" formed by the mythic division of *timai* among the Gods, which parallels the organisation of the polity. In accord with the analogy governing the entire dialogue, esoteric exegesis, as the path to integrity for the Gods in the mythic narrative, is a path to integrity for the mortal soul as well. In so far as we can restore to each God her integrity – her *total* causality – we shall also restore wholeness and providential arrangement to the cosmos, in which everything is disposed somehow on account of the Good. In this manner we shall find our way from the condition of a tripartite soul, with its conflicting faculties carefully harmonized, to the singularity entailed in our choice of a life-pattern.[44] This choice, like the direct narration of the dithyrambic poet (394b–c),

---

43 I have discussed some of the methods of this exegesis in "The Theological Interpretation of Myth," *The Pomegranate: The International Journal of Pagan Studies* 7.1 (2005), 27–41, republished in *Essays on a Polytheistic Philosophy of Religion*.

44 Compare the interpretation of unitary personhood in Plato as an "achievement" rather than an "endowment" in Lloyd P. Gerson, *Knowing Persons: A Study in Plato* (Oxford: Oxford University Press, 2003), with specific reference to tripartition (chapter 3), and a similar view in Mary Margaret McCabe, *Plato's Individuals* (Princeton: Princeton University Press, 1994) that "being a unified person is for Plato … not something I can take for granted … but rather something to which I aspire," (p. 264).

expresses our singular experience of beauty, according to which we choose not just a paradigm for our life alone, but necessarily a paradigm for the cosmos as well, because everything else adjusts itself to our choice. The wholeness of the cosmos is present in each of those souls, not in a totalizing paradigm-of-paradigms belonging to a different order, because the paradigm of the cosmos as a whole is simply Animality, according to the *Timaeus*, and the order possessed by the All is thus simply the order things have as a result of the desires and choices of animals.[45]

In this respect the philosophical cosmogony in the *Timaeus* can on no account be understood in isolation from the role of paradigms throughout the *Republic*, culminating in the life-patterns chosen by souls in the festal meadow in Er's account. I have remarked above that the abundance of paradigms available in the democratic state (557d–e, 561e) shows that for all its flaws the democratic state is ontologically basic in its homology with the eschatological meadow on which the choices of paradigms are laid. But the notorious critique of art as representation or "imitation" (*mimêsis*) is also undercut decisively by Socrates's recourse to the painter (472d) who, "having sketched a paradigm, say of the most beautiful person," cannot reasonably be asked "to demonstrate that such a man could also possibly come to be." The arts, as *representing* reality, cut a poor figure for Plato, since their proper role lies in *forming* it, providing it with paradigms, a role lying on a plane superior not only to the state but to so-called "forms" as well, if by the latter we mean things akin to higher-order analogues of plans for manufactured items (596b). The *true* forms, rather, are those things around which crystallise the experiences of beauty that lend integrity to animal units. In this we see the subordination of eidetics to henology in genuine Platonism. Formal unity, Socrates says, is due either to a God's will (*boulêsis*) or to "some necessity" (*tis anankê*) (597c). It is due to necessity if we understand formal unity as simply given by the power of definition – this is the lower sense of "form", which Plato appropriately exemplifies by an artefact, while form in the higher sense, as in the paradigms of lives, does not

---

45 On the relation between the personal paradigm and the cosmic paradigm, see further the aforementioned "Animal and Paradigm in Plato".

subordinate particulars to a universal. This higher formal unity is due to will, the choice of a whole cosmos by a whole, integral individual. This [**101**] is the highest plane of formalisation, in the *Republic* as in the *Timaeus* (31a), and both thus accord with the remarks in the *Phaedrus* (250b–d) regarding the pre-eminence of Beauty as a kind of transcendental.

The *Timaeus* tells us that the paradigm of the cosmos, Animality, is the paradigm because it is "the most beautiful intelligible" (30d), and that the paradigm cannot thus be a *part* (30c). This is just where the arts fail. Homer is not paradigmatic on account of any of the parts of his creation, but only on account of the *whole*. For instance, he is not master of any of the arts portrayed in his works (*Republic* 599b ff.), because these representations are merely dependent moments of a whole. The danger of narrative is precisely this, that it can foster our passivity (*pathêma*, 602d), that is, the sense in which we are part of a whole, rather than whole ourselves. This applies even to being part of such a noble whole as a "well-ordered polity" (619c–d). Perhaps the paradigmatic moment, so to speak, to illustrate the danger of this peculiarly narrative passivity is the deceptive theophany (381d–e), for a theophany involving mere appearance can only be the appearance of theophany, inviting the reduction of the Gods' manifestations to psychological events, and hence the subordination of the Gods to mere parts of the whole formed by our experience – a psychologistic "subreption", to borrow a Kantian term.

The countervailing quality that we seek to bring out in myths is effectively *musical*, for as Plato says, music has non-epistemic virtues that are "siblings" (*adelpha*) to those found in narrative, both mythic or fabulous (*mythôdeis*) narrative and the "more realistic" (as I would read *alêthinôteroi* here) (522a), and thus prior to this distinction between, as it were, "fiction" and "non-fiction". Though enigmatic, the passage points nevertheless to what must be "saved" in the myth: a direct causal force that can only be impeded by literalism, for literal interpretation opposes the myth to truth, whereas the virtue inherent in narrative cuts across the divide between the "fabulous" and the "truthful". Similarly, the city of guardians divides the world into, e.g., Hellenes and barbarians (470c), which Plato uses at *Statesman* 262d as an example of a faulty division of things, another being the division into "humans" and all other animals.[46] Narrative may not be a form of knowledge, despite the existence of a "science" of symbols; but our reception of its para-epistemic virtue can be thwarted by a pseudo-knowledge that polemicises narrative, pitting truth and fantasy against one another. Myth is neither literal nor allegorical nor psychological, but simply *musically* causal and ontological.

The essential incompleteness of the narrative whole, its inability to exhaustively determine its parts, is inscribed in the city of the guardians itself. This city is a contradiction, framed as a "fevered" city requiring total mobilization to secure and defend a surplus to be consumed by an unproductive elite. This elite, however, is purged from the city as it is being formulated, which thus eliminates its own reason for being. Within the artistic whole of the "city in words", this class of pure consumers is the figure – but a faulty one – of the "user", who is introduced at 601c–d as superior to the "maker" and the "imitator" alike. By subordinating the maker, the demiurge, Plato decisively anticipates – and renders unnecessary – the similar move associated with the "Gnostic" movement. The "user" transcends the paradigm she chooses just by virtue of choosing [**102**] it, but in doing so she is implicated as a part in the whole she has adopted. When the consumer class is eliminated, however, where is the "user" to be found in Plato's portrait of the world, but in those who "run about to all the Dionysiac festivals" and who are in a way "similar to philosophers" (475e)? These bacchants are the only true worldly expression of the pure user, the consumer of appearance itself. Accordingly, they are the structural counterparts of the Apollonian exegete, hermeneutics and the revel being the two roads from the state to the festal city.

If, in eliminating the condition that called for its positing, the city of the guardians has not purged itself of a mere contingency, then it has proven itself possible *only* as a "city in words", as a paradigm envisioned from within the plenitude of

---

46 Compare the notorious equivocation in the *Timaeus* (90e–92c) between the original, paradigmatic "humanity" and the human species, which is merely one of many animal species declined from a generic animality. There is thus a wider and a narrower sense of "human" corresponding to the wider and narrower "goodness", on which again see my "Animal and Paradigm in Plato".

paradigms available in the democratic state, a city of which one may only be a phantasmal citizen (592a–b). The city in words, the city of imagination, plays no genuinely political function except insofar as there is inherent political value in an imaginal citizenship, a passport for the soul proving that the soul is not native in its divided state, its tripartition into consuming, spirited and rational parts. This in turn forms the basis for an art of not being governed in just this way or that, as Foucault defined 'critique'. The proper place of the guardian city lies in the emergence of soul, the psychical city, but that role cannot be representational, fostering imitations; it must be symbolic and musical.[47] Indeed, if the guardian city is nothing other than a symbol for the function of imaginal citizenship, it would be senseless to attempt to institute the city of guardians on the physical plane, for every city is already the city of guardians.

The condition of the soul, in passing from the city of pigs, which is the form of the shared life as such but constitutes only the weakest civic unity, to the city of guardians, the city of hounds and sheep, the beehive city (520b), a city that is "truly *one*", that "consents to be a unity" in itself (423a–b) and is hence its own organism, becomes *mysterious*: the soul is necessarily a *mystês*, one undergoing initiation, in it. Myths with *hyponoiai*, "deep meanings" that conflict with their superficial sense – and let us be clear, this can only mean *all* myths – can only be shared, in the guardian city, with "a very small audience … under a pledge of secrecy and after sacrificing not a pig" – the sacrifice at Eleusis – "but some huge and unprocurable victim" (378a). Instead of a pig, the sacrifice demanded is a citizen of the city of pigs, the surrender of the wholeness of the festal subject. The city of pigs knows no "barbarians", it does not subjugate anyone or treat anything as a mere resource; but the city of the guardians has an outside, beyond its walls, just as "forms" have their "matter" in the war of formation, as Proclus describes it.[48]

---

47 Note the "guardian" class of deities on the intellective plane in the *Platonic Theology* of Proclus, exemplified by the Hellenic Kouretes (book V chaps. 33–5 and 121–31 in Saffrey and Westerink).

48 Proclus speaks of the "war" in which "things that come to be in a foreign place" at one time "by introducing the universal, by means of form dominate the natural substrate," while at another

We see this struggle reflected as well, surprisingly, in some of Socrates's remarks about mathematics, which it turns out is not such a placid study: "the study for which we are seeking must have this additional qualification ... [t]hat it be not useless to soldiers" (521d). With the proper training, these guardians will not be like "irrational lines" (534d) in the state. In the *Laws*, the Hellenes' lack of attention to the issue of irrational number, that is, of incommensurability, renders them "pigs rather than human beings" (*Laws* 819d). The mathematics of irrational number and of incommensurables may be taken "esoterically" as a symbol for the esoteric hermeneutics lying secretly at the heart of the city of guardians, veiled [103] by the divided line, veiled by the *Republic*'s seemingly closed economy of ascent and descent.[49] For the citizens of the city of words *are* on a deeper level "irrational lines", "incommensurable" despite the "noble lie" of autochthony, just as the souls in the netherworld meadow can make no choice pure of their own histories. The thesis that Plato deliberately incorporates irrational numbers as primitive building blocks in the *Timaeus* cosmogony accords well with what is suggested by these passages in the *Republic* and the *Laws*.[50] But Plato was not merely "Pythagorizing", for he recognised the limitations of mathematics narrowly construed, treated as the lesser arithmetic in the *Philebus* (56d–e), in that it abstracts from the differences between different kinds of unit, whereas the "philosopher's arithmetic" will take into account incommensurability, not merely of the sort geometers discovered, but the radical existential incommensurability of

---

time "withdrawing to the particular ... partake of divisibility, weakness ... and division" (*Platonic Theology* I 18.86.5–9). This polemical formation is the key, in particular, to the Platonic exegesis of the *Iliad*, as noted above.

49 One might profitably compare the position of the city of guardians relative to its externalities to that of Euclidean geometry within an implicit non-Euclidean context, as discussed in Vittorio Hösle, "Plato's Foundation of the Euclidean Character of Geometry," pp. 161-182 in Dmitri Nikulin, ed., *The Other Plato: The Tübingen Interpretation of Plato's Inner-Academic Teachings* (Albany: State University of New York Press, 2012).

50 On this thesis, see Denis O'Brien, *Theories of Weight in the Ancient World*, vol. 2 (Leiden: Brill, 1984), pp. 345–9.

which that is the symbol. Like the mythic narrative, the whole cannot synoptically render its parts; the city proves, ultimately, to be nothing other than its perspectives, or rather is itself the hermeneutical or exegetical process by which each makes its mutability and complexity peculiarly her own.

If, as Cicero says, Socrates paints his polity for us "not as possibly existing, but as making it possible that the principle of political things be seen" (*De re publica* 2.52), then I wish to argue that that principle is primarily hermeneutical. The Socratic construction is neither "utopian" nor "anti-utopian", neither possible nor impossible, because it is not a plan but a paradigm, with the mode of being appropriate to *paradeigmata*. As such, the city is not potential but real, but it exists in the labour of interpretation of its citizens, because paradigms, in Plato's sense, exist in being appropriated by individuals in a peculiar, daimonic fashion. A paradigm, once chosen, comes to life, becomes a daimon. This is how it is explained in the eschatological account of Er, which tells how mortal beings choose the *paradeigmata* of the lives they are about to live, and which provides the key for understanding the paradigm of the city that has come before. This city will not come to be through imagining it as it is described, as though it is a representation, but rather through the procedure that is specifically denied to its guardians, namely interpretative work upon myth. This work, guided and guarded by the true principles concerning the Gods, makes it possible for the myths to take soul and ensoul the polity. The city, in turn, is ensouled through its citizens seeking their justice, which ultimately is a unique meaning for one's life, in which fashion the labour of hermeneutics becomes continuous with operative theurgy. Citizenship in this way acquires a special sense which involves the citizen's freedom from any determined role in the social order.

Polytheism and the Euthyphro[*]

ABSTRACT: In this reading of the *Euthyphro*, Socrates and Euthyphro are seen less in a primordial conflict between reason and devotion, than as sincere Hellenic polytheists engaged in an inquiry based upon a common intuition that, in addition to the irreducible agency of the Gods, there is also some irreducible intelligible content to holiness. This reading is supported by the fact that Euthyphro does not claim the authority of revelation for his decision to prosecute his father, but rather submits it to elenchus, and that Euthyphro does not embrace the 'solution' of theological voluntarism when Socrates explicitly offers it. Since the goal of this inquiry is neither to eliminate the noetic content of the holy, nor to eliminate the Gods' agency, the purpose of the elenchus becomes the effort to articulate the results of this productive tension between the Gods and the intelligible on the several planes of Being implied by each conception of the holy which is successively taken up and dialectically overturned to yield the conception appropriate to the next higher plane, a style of interpretation characteristic of the ancient Neoplatonists.

The *Euthyphro* comes at the very beginning of the traditional arrangement of Plato's dialogues—traditional at least as far back

---

[*] This essay originally appeared in *Epoché: A Journal for the History of Philosophy*, Vol. 18, Issue 2 (Spring 2014), pp. 311-323. The pagination from this publication appears in brackets.

as Thrasyllus—and, at least for us, tends to set the stage for the unfolding of Plato's thought, though the relative dearth of attention paid to it in antiquity stands in contrast to the importance assigned to it today. This fact should, indeed, alert us to the possibility that typical modern approaches to the dialogue are motivated by typically modern concerns. It is most well-known for the so-called 'Euthyphro dilemma' it has imparted to the philosophy of religion. This problem is concisely stated in the dialogue at 10a: "Is the holy [*hosios*, also frequently translated 'pious'], holy because it is loved by the Gods, or loved [by them] because it is holy?" Without wishing to discount the significance of the abundant reflections upon this problem in philosophy after antiquity, or to deny that we can see ancient Platonists on many occasions wrestling with the 'Euthyphro problem', albeit not explicitly linked to this dialogue, it would not be unfair, I think, to say that thinkers after antiquity have approached the problem within the framing of monotheism. Some scholars, to be sure, particularly recently, have displayed greater openness than others to situating the [21] piety of Socrates and of Plato *within* Hellenic polytheism, rather than on a trajectory away from it and toward some variety of philosophical monotheism; Mark McPherran and Jon Mikalson, in particular, stand out in this regard. To be open to this requires acknowledging, among other things, that the absence, in a given dialogue or even generally, of explicit affirmations, much less elenctic justifications, of elements utterly basic to the worldview of a Hellenic polytheist cannot be taken as manifesting a lack of support for them. It seems too often as though Socrates is on trial again in the pages of modern scholars who demand from him and from Plato an arbitrarily high threshold of proof that they identify with the tradition of Hellenic polytheism, or define that tradition so narrowly as to ensure that they do not.[51] While in many respects

---

51 Examples of this tendency in the literature abound. For example, Kofi Ackah declares the "dialectical result" of the dialogue up to 11a to be that "piety understood as a relationship between humans and externally existing, fully anthropomorphic gods has no probative basis and is logically incoherent," ("Plato's *Euthyphro* and Socratic Piety," *Scholia* 15 (2006), p. 30), when demanding proof for the existence of the Gods is far from being the goal of this Platonic dialogue; nor is it clear how such

it is quite difficult to say something novel about Plato, in *this* respect, that is, insofar as one would speak about Plato the polytheist, it still is not.[52] This essay is not about polytheism as a mere socio-historical fact in the *Euthyphro*; rather, it concerns the meaning and value of the *Euthyphro* for the polytheistic philosophy of religion. Therefore, I do not intend to concern myself a great deal with the abundant secondary literature on the dialogue, but rather with reading the text, thinking along with it and around it, but informed particularly by hermeneutic strategies characteristic of the Neoplatonists. [**22**]

At stake in the *Euthyphro*, clearly, is the relationship between theology and philosophy. Euthyphro is a diviner, Socrates a philosopher: one of the things we must measure for ourselves is just how great this difference is, and what is its true nature. This difference can be exaggerated. As McPherran points

---

positive ontological results are supposed to be produced from the dialectical procedure. Similarly, Roslyn Weiss argues "that it does not follow from Socrates' engaging in sacrificial rites either that he believes in the gods to whom he sacrifices or that he regards such activity as pious," and even dismisses his final words at *Phaedo* 118a as a "genuine expression of piety," ("Virtue Without Knowledge: Socrates' Conception of Holiness in Plato's *Euthyphro*," *Ancient Philosophy* 14 (1994), p. 272 n. 23.). Weiss takes no account of the testimonies elsewhere in Plato, or in Xenophon, to Socrates' belief in the Hellenic Gods, despite the fact that her thesis concerning the non-epistemic character of Socratic piety would be entirely consistent with sincere participation in the Hellenic theophany. McPherran, at least, does not deem to accuse Socrates of having forsworn his several civic oaths, "all of which called the gods of the state as witnesses" ("Does Piety Pay? Socrates and Plato on Prayer and Sacrifice," p. 95).

52 "Still" in the sense that there are definite indications of positive movement toward at least the openness I described, Gerd Van Riel's *Plato's Gods* (Farnham: Ashgate, 2013) being a prominent example. My reference to Plato here, rather than to Socrates and Plato, represents an initial acknowledgement that I see Plato's depiction of Socrates in the so-called "early" dialogues as part of a theoretical continuum with Plato's "late" metaphysics, and not as a categorically different undertaking.

out,[53] Socrates' interactions with his *daimonion* do share certain traits with divination, and Socrates does upon occasion speak of himself as a sort of lay *mantis* (e.g., *Phaedo* 85b; *Phaedrus* 242c). Euthyphro, for his part, is akin to Socrates in more than just the ways he cites himself at the beginning of the dialogue, and of which modern readers are too derisive. It should not be, after all, an affront for Euthyphro to express such a kinship.[54] Moreover, since the later antique Platonic tradition regarded the etymologies *à la* Euthyphro in the *Cratylus* (396d & sqq.) not as mocking, but as sincere, the notion that Socrates and Euthyphro have each something to learn from the other is not outlandish. In this sense, we may see Euthyphro and Socrates as engaged in the same work, broadly conceived: namely, out of a personally experienced sense of divine vocation, trying to grasp for themselves, and not merely through passive participation in the social dimension of cult, something about the nature of the Gods and about the nature of the cosmos as the Gods would know it. Hence Proclus[55] sees Socrates in the *Cratylus* as mediating between Euthyphro's "imaginative" (*phantastikos*) and passively given (*boskêmatôdeis*, literally as of what is fed to domesticated animals) conceptions about the Gods, and his own characteristically "scientific" (*epistêmonikos*) understanding, by assuming a "doxastic" mode in the *Cratylus* etymologies, one, that is, in which there is at once that which is the object of belief or *doxa*, such as the proper names of Gods who are the objects

---

53 "Socratic Reason and Socratic Revelation," *Journal of the History of Philosophy* 29.3, July 1991, pp. 345-373.
54 One interesting commonality between them not cited by Euthyphro himself is a strong concern with purification. While commentators have often remarked upon Euthyphro's concern with *miasma* as exceptional, typically in support of arguments that Euthyphro's religious orientation lies outside the mainstream of Athenian religious life, somewhere on the "Orphic" spectrum (e.g. Kahn, "Was Euthyphro the Author of the Derveni Papyrus", pp. 56-7), they have not tended to relate this to Socrates' own conception of elenchus as "a kind of ritual purification of the soul," (McPherran, *Religion of Socrates*, p. 152), and to the (much debated) "Orphic" aspects of Plato's own thought.
55 *In Platonis Cratylum Commentaria*, ed. Pasquali, pp. 67.24-68.9.

of experience and religious regard, *and also* intellectual insight, as we see in the interpretation Socrates develops from examining the names of the Gods as modified words or strings of words. In this doxastic labor Socrates recovers from the names given to the Gods in the theophanic experience of the ancients that moment of cognitive and intelligible *response* to theophany that embodies, inseparably, the presence of the Gods and of the human agent *together* in the encounter. [23]

The contrast between Socrates and Euthyphro against a shared background of common effort is echoed in something Socrates says at 3d, namely that Euthyphro is not in danger of prosecution from the people because he does not impart his wisdom (*sophia*) to others, or rather, we might say, that as a diviner Euthyphro shares only the *results* of his inquiry. Socrates is ironic, or perhaps merely polite, in attributing to Euthyphro a wisdom withheld, when the wisdom in question can only be attributed, first, to the Gods themselves, and second, to the one who can arrive at an adequate *interpretation* of what is conveyed to the diviner, and through them to a wider public. Even if Euthyphro possessed the wisdom to interpret the results of his divination, this would bear an ambiguous relationship his job description, so to speak, as a diviner.[56]

It must be said, in this connection, that Euthyphro never claims in the dialogue to have been specifically directed by the Gods to do anything. Can we, then, simply *assume* that Euthyphro is acting as a result of some kind of divination? I do not see how we can. It is, rather, Euthyphro's father who is explicitly said to have sought out a religious adviser (*exêgêtês*, 4c). Even if we accept that Euthyphro would regard himself as an exegete adequate for his own purposes, Euthyphro simply does

---

56 See Aaron Landry, "Inspiration and Τέχνη: divination in Plato's *Ion*," *Plato Journal* 14 (2014), pp. 85-97 for a nuanced treatment of the issue of the diviner's knowledge. Even Theoclymenus, Socrates' example of possession divination, from *Odyssey* 20.351-7, is able to interpret his divination (20.367-70) (pp. 90-1); and Diotima, from the *Symposium*, is at once diviner and philosopher (pp. 92-3). See also chap. 3, "Divination and its Range of Influence," in Jon D. Mikalson, *Greek Popular Religion in Greek Philosophy* (Oxford: Oxford University Press, 2010), pp. 110-139.

not ever frame his decision in a manner that presents it as the result of any kind of divination. All that we can see from what is on the page is that Euthyphro has *inferred* his responsibilities through analogy with myths. Plato therefore does not stage in this text a direct confrontation between reason and revelation. It would have been awkward, no doubt, for Euthyphro to say that he had been directed to this course of action by a God, and for Socrates to proceed to interrogate that revelation, especially since, as McPherran points out,[57] Socrates speaks in his own case of receiving divine direction from divination and from dreams, as well as from his divine sign or *daimonion*. However, as McPherran goes on to argue, Socrates does nevertheless have a way open to him to criticize any given interpretation Euthyphro offers of the revelation he has received without resorting to impiety, and we ought not assume that Plato felt incapable of presenting such an inquiry in a suitable fashion. Indeed, the manner in which the discussion proceeds would seem to suggest that Euthyphro is not to be understood as acting on a specific divine direction, but rather on a general conception of what counts as pious behavior, [24] a conception which is in broad terms within the boundaries of what generally counts as piety among his peers, though his application of these norms has led to a result that will surprise those peers.[58] This makes the move to an inquiry into the *nature of piety* a natural one—in fact, a move that Euthyphro has already implicitly made himself. In this respect, we may class Euthyphro among those clergy of whom we read in the *Meno* that Socrates has had conversation, inasmuch as they wish to give a reasoning account of their ministry (*Meno* 81a). Or at least, that Euthyphro has a tendency in this direction, inasmuch as he seems to have a certain inchoate sense that reasoning should play some role in his religious life,

---

57 "Socratic Reason and Socratic Revelation," p. 351.

58 Jon D. Mikalson, *Honor Thy Gods: Popular Religion in Greek Tragedy* (Chapel Hill, NC: University of North Carolina Press, 1991), pp. 198-201, argues persuasively that "Euthyphro's concept of piety" as displayed in the dialogue, "echoes similar thoughts found throughout Greek tragedy," and that "scattered and fragmentary parallels for Euthyphro's ideas appear in other sources for popular religion," hence "his conception of piety was not idiosyncratic" (201).

even beyond the necessity for interpreting his direct communications from the Gods, so that his piety can inform even those decisions he makes *without* recourse to divination. In this respect, it may be significant that it is within the time it takes for his father's messenger to seek out the advice of the exegete that his hired man dies, though the death is directly caused by his father's negligence (4d). Nor are we told the result of the consultation with the exegete. It seems that Plato feels no need to even provide the materials for a confrontation between reason and revelation as such.

Most notably in this respect, when given the opportunity by Socrates to render his stated beliefs mutually consistent by straightforwardly affirming that holiness just *is* an effect of divine will, Euthyphro does not do so, clearly wishing to preserve the noetic integrity of the notion of holiness (10a-c). What troubles Euthyphro, or at least perhaps does so once Socrates has pointed it out, is that he has no *rational* means for adjudicating between two conflicting pious duties: reverence for the law, and reverence for his father, whom he would prosecute under the law. Euthyphro's intention is to prosecute his father as the law would demand, and he sees this as following from a universal, implicitly rational maxim that the law should apply to everyone equally (4b). We know from *Gorgias* 480c that Socrates does in fact agree that one should try to see ones friends and family prosecuted if they have done wrong. But how has Euthyphro gotten to this recognition? He doesn't seek to justify this maxim, or his intended actions, through reason, or at any rate, only through a particular kind of reasoning, namely arguing that for him to prosecute his father in this fashion honors a principle established by the Gods when, for example, Zeus overthrows Kronos. We should not be too quick to dismiss this line of thought. Analogy is a form of reasoning, and the transition from the reign of Kronos to [25] that of Zeus as recounted in Hesiod does lead to the establishment of a more just order among the Gods, one chiefly operating through persuasion and the balancing of honors (*timai*) rather than force of will (Ouranos) or calculation (Kronos).

Euthyphro's application of analogy implies that a principle can be univocally applied to Gods and to humans, despite their different ontological status: "they are inconsistent in what they say about the Gods and about me" (6a). This again suggests that

Euthyphro is really seeking, whether he recognizes it or not, an exercise of reason that would transcend the division between humans and the Gods. Nor does Euthyphro see a *symbolic* interpretation of the myth, even though he emphasizes to Socrates the supra-rational nature of the events treated in myths. For when Socrates expresses doubt that there could really be war between Gods, Euthyphro characterizes such truths as "marvelous" and "astonishing" (6b, c), but does not draw the further conclusion that just insofar as these mythic events are *mysterious* that they might *not* therefore provide simple, unproblematic analogies to human behavior. Daniel Werner's recent study, "Myth and the Structure of Plato's *Euthyphro*,"[59] though highlighting the importance for the dialogue of Euthyphro's "adherence to traditional myth," fails to even recognize the possibility of a pious *and* symbolic hermeneutic of myth beyond the simplistic opposition of *mythos* and *logos*. The issue cannot be reduced, as Werner would wish, to a matter of an "acceptance" or "rejection" of traditional myths, or of whether "acceptance" of the myths is "loose" or "wholesale" (p. 46). Mythic reception is hardly so simple. We should not assume that Plato would be averse to a symbolic hermeneutic of myth. In the critique of mythic poetry in the *Republic*, myths requiring esoteric (or "hyponoetic", *Rep.* 378d) interpretation are not suitable for unmediated, simplistic application, which is why it is questionable to impart such myths to children, who are not capable of advanced theology, or to inhabitants of a "fevered" city whose state of total mobilization, a permanent state of emergency, may render them similarly impaired. Such symbolic interpretation has as its guiding principle, not the reduction of "irrational" myth to some purified *logos*, but the pious regard for the Gods as being "each the most beautiful and best thing possible" (*Rep.* 381c).

Insofar as problematic myths like these shed light in particular upon the *ontological difference* between humans and Gods, however, it may well be these myths that interest us most of all. To guide us in their interpretation, however, we shall need philosophical, ontological tools. Once these were developed within Platonic schools, the interpretation of such myths

---

59 *International Philosophical Quarterly* Vol. 52, No. 1, Issue 205 (March 2012), pp. 41-62.

flourished, not in a defensive posture, but rather for the genuine ontological value such myths have to offer.[60] But in the *Euthyphro*, the difference between humans and Gods is [**26**] approached obliquely, through a series of hypotheses about the nature of holiness all of which have a domain of valid application, but all of which also contain some seed of their dialectical reversal, which will urge us further along in a manner that, in fact, sketches for us the outlines of the structure of being. This, at any rate, is the style of positive interpretation of dialogical refutation favored in the later Platonic schools, and which serves us better than other interpretive hypotheses with respect to this dialogue, if we do not assume that Plato intends to portray Socrates as overturning, rather than merely refining, popular conceptions of piety.[61]

The essential question in the *Euthyphro*, and in the Platonic approach to theology generally, I would argue, is the relationship between the singular (the unique or "peculiar") and the common. When Euthyphro chooses to treat the events of myth just like worldly events, and looks to define holiness according to what the Gods choose, he chooses in favor of the singularity of the Gods as individuals, rather than orienting himself to divine *attributes*. He affirms the integrity of the Gods by affirming the unique, unrepeatable nature of the mythic event, which can offer a paradigm for practice precisely insofar as it does *not* depend upon some further principle which it merely instantiates, and which would therefore demand a prior elucidation. At the same time, he searches for a universality which would not compromise singularity.

From the perspective of later Platonic philosophy of religion, Euthyphro indeed shows the proper instincts at least, in that he wishes *both* to secure the ontological priority of henadic individuals (the unique Gods) to the eidetic or formal in its entirety *and* to pursue an *eidos* of the holy—for Euthyphro does not accept the proffered voluntarism in which the holy would be

---

60 See, e.g., Lamberton, *Homer the Theologian*; Struck, *Birth of the Symbol.*
61 See Mikalson (2010) for an extended defense of the mainstream nature of at least some version of all of the models of piety proposed in the *Euthyphro*.

holy purely by virtue of the Gods' having chosen it. We do not have to assume that, as R. E. Allen would have it, Euthyphro is simply a theological voluntarist who misunderstands his own position.[62] Rather, we can see Euthyphro as experiencing a legitimate pull in both directions, and that preserving and articulating this tension, rather than collapsing it into one pole or the other, is the Platonist's legitimate aim as well. This tension can be seen as driving the *Euthyphro*'s dialectic.

Euthyphro realizes in an inchoate fashion that affirming divine individuality—and, inherently, plurality—ought not lead to a skeptical or nominalistic rejection of the eidetic altogether. "Holiness" ought to have *something* [27] common to it, though he is correct to reject that such a common substance—or a common substance for any of the virtues—will subordinate the Gods *existentially*, and Plato does not press such a conclusion, either. The Good, rather, as we will see from the *Republic*, is beyond substance (*ousia*), which in the later development of Platonism was elucidated, in conjunction with the henology of Plato's *Parmenides*, as expressing the primacy of the unitary or singular (*heniaios*), of individual existence (*hyparxis*), over the ideal or formal.[63] Hence the "Euthyphro problem" is really that of how the common emerges from the singular. The singulars "down here", so to speak, everyday units, may indeed be ontologically posterior in many ways to the forms they participate, but the *ultimate* singulars, the Gods, eternally *generate* their community. Moreover, even if we had no Gods, we would have to be able to at least conceive such autonomously good agents in order to secure the metaphysical possibility of freedom. It solves nothing to either reduce these agents to arbitrary, and hence unfree choices, *or* to a good which arbitrarily chooses them.

We see a reflection of this problem of peculiarity in the discussion of conflicts among the Gods (7b-d). Insofar as the conflicts between the Gods are understood to be *peculiar* to each, they lack, by definition, objective resolutions. In this way they

---

62 *Plato's Euthyphro and the Earlier Theory of Forms: A Reinterpretation of the Republic* (Abingdon, Oxon: Routledge, 1970 [repr. 2013]), p. 44.
63 Cf. "Polytheism and Individuality in the Henadic Manifold," *Dionysius* Vol. 23, 2005, pp. 83-104.

are like disputes over the Good among us, which in our case produce enmity (7d). This is not to say that enmity results in the divine case, and Socrates would certainly reject that it does. But when the conflicts among the Gods are understood as strife among absolutely unique individuals, all of whose attributes are also taken as wholly unique to each of them, there can necessarily be no formalization of the conflict as embodying a conflict of objective principles that might therefore be mediated. Dispute on this plane, the plane of pure singulars, is always a dispute over each separate act (8e), and any resolution will also be unique. Hence for us as well, when we take ourselves existentially, that is, as singulars, each problem of the application of principles is occurring as it were for the first time, every time. If Euthyphro is going to stay on the plane of singulars—which is in one respect a *low* plane of being, when it pertains to singulars such as us, but in another respect *the highest*, when it pertains to *a priori* singulars such as Gods—then only a *singular* judgment, such as an act of divination, can justify his act.

Euthyphro does not resort to this, however, inasmuch as he continues to accept Socrates' challenge to him to produce *universality*, something that can be affirmed as true of *all the Gods*, without restriction, and hence something true of them *qua* Gods. This is the breakthrough in which we are invited to participate: an inquiry into the Gods as a *kind* of thing, with an essential nature, a nature of Godhood. At the beginning of the Platonic enterprise, therefore, we are advised [28] that the inquiry will extend even this far. But where we mistake the enterprise is in seeing its end as placing a reified essence prior to the existence of the Gods, or, for that matter, affirming a wholesale subordination of other individuals to the Idea. Moreover, what prevents the latter is precisely that very Platonic piety which will not subordinate the Gods in this fashion. Hence other singulars are saved, too, in varying degrees, and with a status doubtless "problematic", by that philosophical piety which saves the Gods. Saving the singulars *is the problem*, and this is what recognizing Platonic piety, not toward the Idea, but toward the *immortals*, and toward the possibility of fellowship with them in and through our mortal being, allows us in turn to understand about the entire Platonic project.[64]

---

64 I have developed this at further length through a reading of

The dialectical ascent, then, begins in earnest from 10a-c, where Socrates poses to Euthyphro the question of whether he wishes to regard holiness as simply a passive quality of things resulting from their having been chosen by the Gods. That it should be merely an implicitly arbitrary choice and a resulting *pathos* of something, rather than a relationship more fundamental and even in some way constitutive for both, is the bottom, baseline position, but one which also, if we read it proleptically, reflects, just by virtue of being the lowest, something of the pure causal activity of the highest principle, for the Gods as the ultimate agents will indeed, in the ultimate development of antique Platonism, possess this sheer sovereignty over Being in the last analysis. Conceiving of the holy in this fashion would also be consistent with the Platonic doctrine regarding *powers*, and therefore would conceive that which is holy as the receptacle of divine power. Thus in the *Republic* (477c-d), we read that powers (*dynameis*) can be discriminated in no other way than by that to which they are relative and by that which comes about through them.[65] A power, thus, has no intrinsic character but what it is in that which it effects, and thus this putative definition of holiness may be regarded as the "power" definition. Powers are therefore, in themselves, pure relations, and holiness the pure power of relation to the Gods, without any further intelligible determination, as *transcending* the intelligible. The proper understanding of the ontological status of the powers of the Gods lies on the far side of the investigation Socrates and Euthyphro are now undertaking, however, not to mention on the far side of the historical development of Platonism in antiquity. Therefore, Euthyphro correctly refuses to stay at this position as it is prereflectively articulated, and not ripe to be grasped, even though it would be [**29**] consistent with the intuition of the sovereign power of divine choice. He wishes,

---

the *Phaedrus* and *Symposium* in "Plato's Gods and the Way of Ideas," *Diotima: Review of Philosophical Research* 39, 2011 (Hellenic Society for Philosophical Studies, Athens), pp. 73-87.
65 Cf. Hans-Georg Gadamer's discussion of this doctrine in "The Dialectic of the Good in the *Philebus*," pp. 117-118 in *The Idea of the Good in Platonic-Aristotelian Philosophy*, trans. P. Christopher Smith (New Haven: Yale University Press, 1986).

instead, to pursue the *choiceworthiness* of that which the Gods choose.

In addition to the desire for a substantial notion of the holy, however, Socrates points out a problem forcing the ascent, by posing the question of fear and reverence at 12a-b. We have reverence for something in regard to a virtue it possesses, while we fear something simply because of its action or possible action upon us; and yet insofar as reverence is a part (*meros*) of fear (12c), we see again the emergence of something with eidetic content from out of something conceived as a pure relation. Socrates thus presents Euthyphro with another implicit figuration of divine production.

The structural consideration with respect to fear and reverence leads Socrates in turn to the notion of holiness as a part of justice, as reverence is a kind of fear. Now it is a question, not of something structurally homologous to the relation between the Gods and the (eidetically) holy, but of something that might begin to speak to the nature of holiness itself. The question of piety as a part of justice concerns the place that piety, the activities specifically directed toward the Gods in devotion (*therapeia*), has in the system of the cosmos, of the total well-ordering of things. It takes up again the purely interactional or relational conception of the holy as that which is chosen by or beloved of the Gods. This conception is enriched, however, through recognizing that holiness thus conceived is an attribute, not of the holy thing in isolation, but of an economy of devotion. It represents an advance in this respect. But given its wide-reaching significance, how can this economy be just one part of the whole of justice, just one activity among the many activities of necessity and of choice that fill up a life?

This question concerns the status of the Gods as a particular class among beings, a portion of the cosmos. Eventually Platonists will come to recognize [**30**] that the Gods cannot just be certain things among all other things. Hence, at the beginning of this journey, Socrates asks the *aim* of attending to the Gods. It cannot have as its aim supplying some need, and hence making the Gods *better* in some way (13c-d). This would be the case if the Gods were solely part of the cosmic system, immanent in it without remainder. There is something limited and misleading, therefore, about the economic model, at least if we understand it as a crude exchange. To every stage of the dialectic corresponds some belief or practice which the dialectical progression does not demand be abandoned, but for which rather it poses a problem, and solving this problem will save what is true in it. The priestesses and priests mentioned in the *Meno*, like Diotima in the *Symposium*, were not looking for something to supersede their devotional works, but for a way of articulating the relationship of these acts to the world.

If Socrates is holding the Gods' transcendence—at least partially or in some respect—of the cosmic economy in his pocket, so to speak, this is not at any rate an insight available to Euthyphro. The next step in the dialectic, accordingly, comes with Euthyphro's substitution of a sublimated economy for the crude one based on need: service (*hypêretikê*) to the Gods in pursuit of their work (*ergon*) (13d-e). The importance of the relationship of service to the Gods is emphasized by its reemergence at a crucial moment in the *Parmenides* (134d-e), where the mastery-and-service relationship between the Gods and ourselves, insofar as it parallels the relationship between the forms and our knowledge of them, poses what is termed the "greatest difficulty" with respect to the theory of forms, if it be poorly understood, for it implies that "we do not rule the Gods with our authority, nor do we know anything of the divine with our knowledge, and by the same reasoning, the Gods likewise, being Gods, are not our masters and have no knowledge of human affairs," (134e, trans. Fowler, mod.).

In the Platonic consideration of the economy of mastery and service, we glimpse the economy of recognition that Hegel would articulate so many centuries later. The difficulty of this relationship, embodied in Euthyphro's inability to say what is the work of the Gods in which we serve them, lies in the fact that there are relationships the very *idea* of which makes necessary reference to that which lies outside the realm of the *ideal*. It is not simply that we lack the knowledge we would need to assist the Gods properly in their work, but rather of conceiving, in the first place, a work as common to them and to us. Knowledge in itself is the grasp of the formal by something not solely formal, namely the soul; so too, the *mastery* exercised by the Gods over us involves essentially entities which in a certain respect would not *exist* for them. Hence, we do not see ourselves in the myths. We may *analogize* ourselves to figures in the myths, as Euthyphro does when he analogizes himself to Zeus and his father to

Kronos, or, more humbly, as when we see ourselves in the mortals portrayed in myth, but we are not straightforwardly there, in that world. Those mortals, too, can only be the object of analogy. In this way, there is something [**31**] in the devotional economy that transcends the economy of myth, which like the economy of the ideas or forms is fundamentally intellective. Here we see how a simplistic opposition of *mythos* and *logos* cannot do justice to the labors of Plato and Platonists. Myths have two faces, one of which looks back to the singularity of the Gods and of revelation, the other of which looks forward to hermeneutic exegesis and the ideas which emerge from it. The limitation of analogy lies in its potential obstruction of the recognition of the procession of being, with its necessary moment of *disanalogy*. Devotion must incorporate the alterity that makes it possible for Gods and mortals to recognize one another in the full alterity of their divergent existential conditions.

From the holy as simple object of divine intention, Socrates and Euthyphro passed on to the notion of a devotional economy of holiness, which has now been refined implicitly from the gross economy of exchange to the sublimated economy of recognition. This economy of recognition transcends even the plane by which the Gods give form to the cosmos, namely the plane of mythic relationships and reciprocal action *within* the divine sphere. The economy of devotion, properly understood, therefore, transcends the economy of demiurgy. This would have to be the case for polytheism not to collapse into intellectualized cosmotheism, and for piety as a distinct activity to disappear. This is the recognition entailed in the reformulation McPherran offers of the conception of divine service in response to Socrates' forceful hint at 14c that Euthyphro has come very near the solution to the nature of holiness before turning aside.[66] For McPherran, the positive Socratic conception of piety is accordingly "that part of justice that is a service of humans to gods, assisting the gods in their primary task to produce their most beautiful product." But we can see that something has dropped out of consideration in order to formulate this definitive statement, which is both *action-based* and focused purely on *human* action. This is a serviceable definition

66 "Piety, Justice, and the Unity of Virtue," *Journal of the History of Philosophy* 38.3 (July 2000), pp. 302-3.

of piety as a human virtue or activity, but not, it would seem, of *holiness* as embodying, or at least *including*, the choiceworthiness of the objects of *divine* choice. This latter, rather, has been pushed back out of view, implicit in the notion of the Gods' "task". For what makes something a task of the Gods? Is it simply that They have taken it up, or is it the task's intrinsic value?

Accordingly, when the difference between humans and Gods is elided, at least aspirationally, in Plato's *Republic*, the discrete virtue of piety vanishes altogether into that of justice, which is simply the proper *adjustment* of powers in the soul, in society, and in the cosmos to one another.[67] There is a sense in which everything, simply by fulfilling its nature and playing out its role in the [**32**] cosmic system, is holy or is expressing piety, but does the attempt to define piety truly dissolve it? Or perhaps the worship of the Gods is something really distinct in itself, but is nevertheless undertaken purely for the sake of the cosmos? This is the position suggested by the notion that piety is "the science [*epistêmê*] of sacrifice and prayer" (14c), the object of which is to "bring salvation to individual families and to states" (14b). The way in which this position is described, both in its recourse to a notion of science, and in its salvific application not to the individual as such, but to greater social units, suggest that it is the highest point achieved by the intellectualized conception of piety, insofar as the latter will only with difficulty recognize the particular, by a process of determining "down" to it by increasingly finer sortal "nets". Salvation, at any rate, as the product of devotion, is indicated by Socrates to be very close (14c) to the solution of the problem of what holiness or piety is with respect to its intelligible content, unless the nearness he indicates, but does not specify, is instead the notion of service in a noble work. Or can it be both, in the sense that the state of our souls in our disposition toward the Gods, that is, the *pure relation* among Gods and mortals, is itself the work, to which of necessity we are peculiarly qualified?

A relationship of *justice* toward the Gods is paradoxical to the degree that they do not need anything from us, and cannot be bettered by our attentions to them (15a-b), even if a beautiful

---

67 Cf. McPherran, "Piety, Justice, and the Unity of Virtue," pp. 324-5, 326-7.

work could be achieved by them and ourselves in concert. They must therefore *in themselves* remain in some respect outside the economy of reciprocal benefit that they underwrite. Even justice most widely and sensitively conceived will thus fall short in capturing what piety is, though it can go a very long way. The very best account we can give of religious life in terms of reciprocal exchange (*do ut des*), even refined to the ultimate degree, still lets something escape. The Gods, to exist in the way the Hellenic tradition intuitively grasps them—because we must recognize that Socrates at no time in this dialogue, or elsewhere, really, introduces novel, controversial premises concerning the Gods, but at most sets the consequences of one intuition against another—must not exist solely in the economy of piety, and therefore the inquiry into the nature of piety has run its course, with the Gods Themselves as its remainder and its precondition. But piety's epistemological virtue is just that this immanent inquiry should reveal the objects of its peculiar concern in this light: the Gods would be of all things what concretely instantiates such self-sufficiency.

The course of this dialectic has therefore proceeded along two tracks, one explicit, in which an intelligible content has been sought for holiness or piety, the progress of which has at every stage also revealed a corresponding, *implicit* conception of piety, in which the holy is so inseparable from divine activity itself as to escape any intelligible framing we might design for it. The circle to which Socrates refers, then, at 15b-c, is not a vicious one, unless we are [**33**] convinced that it is a failure to have elucidated the series of meanings attributable to piety, their sufficiencies and insufficiencies, and also to recognize in the end that there is something more than intelligible embedded in the concept. In this respect, Socrates' reference to his ancestor Daidalos suggests not merely that the argument has gotten away from Euthyphro, but the magic of ensoulment showing itself and arising through the effort at understanding. It is true that in a certain respect, when Socrates urges Euthyphro to "begin again at the beginning" with him (15c), the putative positive conception of piety discerned by McPherran at 14b has been undermined. The notion of service to the Gods in support of a work of theirs has only a relative stability; to return again to the beginning is to return to the motor that has driven the dialectic all along, namely the creative tension between the impulse to

71

compromise none of the Gods' agency, and the understanding that the Gods, being Gods, must have a will that is good, too, and hence this goodness is there to be found in the choices they make.

Euthyphro is often treated with rather more scorn by modern commentators than Socrates' other interlocutors, despite the fact that none of them hold up particularly well to Socrates' scrutiny. Some of this, I believe, is attributable to a bias against Euthyphro's religiosity, which is bound to please neither the atheist nor the monotheist. Euthyphro, in any case, as I have remarked, deserves credit for one thing, at least: he never seeks to jettison the notion of some intelligible content for the concept of the holy. He tries, instead, to hold together the search for this intelligibility and his intuition that there is something irreducible in the relationship to the living Gods. In this, Euthyphro shows himself a true Hellene, we may say, in refusing to divorce the Gods from the world and from reason, nor divorce *these* from the Gods. Whatever transcendence is accorded the Gods, it will not be of the sort that Kierkegaard demands for his God, namely the suspension of all rational and moral claims in the face of the divine command.

For failing to adopt this Kierkegaardian solution, or the alternative of an intellectualized piety refined virtually to the point of atheism, Euthyphro is branded a shallow thinker who cannot see clearly enough to embrace either "genuine" theology or rationality. But in refusing this dichotomy, Euthyphro remains true to the fundamental theological intuitions of his culture, and I would argue that Socrates and Plato would not wish him to do otherwise. Euthyphro may not be a gifted dialectician, but his project is theirs as well, a project in which the transcendence of the Gods in Hellenic theology will ground the cosmos and our free exercise of reason, not suspend it. It's not insignificant, in this light, that Euthyphro seeks divine sanction for recourse to the Athenian justice system, and his transgressiveness lies solely in that he would allow the law to be applied within his family, rather than shielding them.

Socrates, however, has by the end of the dialogue shown it to be thoroughly [**34**] problematic to attempt to justify social action by recourse to theology. But this is because Euthyphro has tried to do so, as it were, without the Gods themselves. Euthyphro tries to match mythic incidents to worldly problems as simple precedents, a portion of myth to a part of the world, but this part-to-part correspondence will undermine the whole-to-whole relationship of the Gods to the social and the cosmic order, the same whole-to-whole relationship that any living thing has to the cosmos, for the Gods are for Euthyphro and Socrates alike living immortals, and not abstract principles or mere formulae that can be applied indifferently, in their personal absence. But this does not leave only divination, on the one hand, and a godless reason on the other, a dichotomy alien, I believe, to the mainstream of Hellenic thinkers.[68] Socrates' own piety, on the testimony of Plato and of Xenophon alike, argues rather for an integration of reason and revelation in a unified soteriology.

---

68 Even Werner, in an account otherwise hostile to Hellenic theology, recognizes that Euthyphro's rejection of the voluntarism Socrates offers him is at least in part due to the fact that "Nowhere in the traditional myths are the gods represented as the sort of beings who definitively establish the nature of right and wrong (or pious and impious) simply through a decree or fiat," (p. 50).

Toward a New Conception of Platonic Henology

ABSTRACT: This essay joins diverse themes in Plato's thought and in a selection of recent scholarship on Plato and Aristotle under a common rubric of inquiry into individuation and the formal theory of manifolds. 'The One' in henology thus understood is no longer a reified (and theoretically otiose) unity. Instead, the Platonic 'One' is nothing other than the diverse conceptions of unity and modes of individuation informing different henological practices or modes of analysis.

Aristotle states that Plato, like the Pythagoreans, took "the One" or "Unity" to be a substance, rather than a predicate (*Met.* 987b22-4). But does Aristotle's point here concern how Plato posits a singular entity called "the One", an entity of which Aristotle may go on to question whether it has *ousia* or does not? That is, do Plato and Aristotle have a dispute within ontology, a dispute about *what there is*, or is it a question instead of the relationship between two different fundamental orientations for philosophy, namely the science of essence nascent in Aristotle, and a different kind of inquiry, a *henology* grounded in the modes of unity and multiplicity?

I do not mean to say that one may not read Plato ontologically, that is, for an account of what entities there are, though I suggest that attempts to do so have blocked a more productive appropriation of his thought. Nor do I suggest that one may not read Aristotle 'henologically' himself. In particular, Edward C. Halper has pursued a reading of the *Metaphysics* for which Aristotle's method is fundamentally henological. Halper, to be clear, does not use the term 'henology' or use the term 'ontology' in the way I do; but he states explicitly that the two main metaphysical issues for Aristotle, namely "whether metaphysics exists as a science," and second "what its first principles and causes are," are both addressed by Aristotle as "one/many issues,"[69] and that Aristotle "supports his main doctrines of being and *ousia*"—in my terms, his ontology—"by showing that they, and they alone, resolve various manifestations of the one/many problem."[70]

For Halper's Aristotle, however, "although metaphysical method involves unity and although the problem of metaphysics is a problem of unity, what emerges from the science is not primarily a doctrine of unity."[71] A comparison may be made here with the distinction noted in Aristotle by Alan Code between a "general essentialism" and Aristotle's "particular theory of substance". Aristotle attempts to show that his particular theory of substance "satisfies the conditions of adequacy for being the focal point in an account of being,"[72] that is, conditions required for any metaphysics. Halper, too, speaks of two "inquiries" in Aristotle, an "inquiry into being" and an "inquiry into *ousia*," to the former of which belongs a broad conception of *ousia*, so that, for instance, mathematicals may be treated as *ousiai* with their own attributes, as the mathematician does, while for the latter, which concerns *ousia* in a narrower sense, mathematicals must be regarded as *attributes* of *ousiai*.[73] To this broader inquiry belong as well the referents of metaphysical terms such as "cause", "genus", "element", "same", "other", "like", "unlike", "contrariety" or, indeed, "one", which since they have "essences

---

69 E. C. Halper, *One and Many in Aristotle's Metaphysics: Books Alpha-Delta* (Las Vegas: Parmenides Publishing, 2009): 8.
70 Halper 2009: 25.
71 Halper 2009: 473.
72 A. Code, "The Philosophical Significance of the Middle Books of Aristotle's Metaphysics," *University of Dayton Review* 19.3 (1988/9), 81-91: 82.
73 Halper 2009: 502.

of another sort" Halper characterizes as "non-categorial essences".[74]

If we see Plato as chiefly concerned with this more general sort of inquiry, we are less likely to find ourselves confused by Plato's apparent comfort with the plurality of inconsistent ontological commitments that would arise from accepting the several hypotheses of the *Parmenides*. Lambros Couloubaritsis thus argues for an interpretation of the *Parmenides* that, while it resists the Neoplatonic systematization of the hypotheses into "un système théologique formé par une hierarchie de principes divins … qui à la fois fondent et expliquent toutes les choses et toutes les activités du réel," that is, an ontology, in the sense I am using it, nevertheless does not take them "comme un jeu." Rather, Couloubaritsis says, Plato uses the hypotheses to establish "différentes *pratiques* de l'Un qui pourraient s'accorder à tel ou tel problème, sans devoir nécessairement former un système rigoureux, ni même un ordre logique déductif."[75] One may therefore distinguish between the production of an ontic hierarchy of principles out of the hypotheses, which must be regarded in some sense as an ontological *reduction*, and the attempt to preserve a relatively acentric or polycentric sense to the hypotheses as yielding a series of henological practices or problematics.

It seems that it was Plato, then, who first effectively, if not explicitly, distinguished henology and ontology. As Mary M. McCabe has remarked, the first part of the *Parmenides*, that is, the discussion between the young Socrates and first Zeno, then Parmenides, has "an explicit ontological commitment to the contrast between forms and particulars," while the second part, namely the several hypotheses, is "free of ontological commitment".[76] That ontological commitments may be *generated* by the hypotheses, as they were by later Platonists, is beside the point. As Couloubaritsis has noted, however, "le danger de

---

74 Halper 2009: 69.

75 L. Couloubaritsis, "De la pratique de l'Un d'Aristote à la formation de la science moderne," in *De la science à la philosophie: Y a-t-il une unité de la connaissance?* Ed. M. Cazenave (Paris: Albin Michel, 2004), 379-421: 389.

76 M. M. McCabe, *Plato's Individuals* (Princeton: Princeton University Press, 1999): 105.

l'appropriation actuelle du terme 'hénologie' ... réside dans sa réduction à une thématique unique et crypto-théologique, qui se résume dans un Un qui se situerait au-delà de l'être."[77] The only real defense against this danger lies in grasping the practical or methodological significance of henology that lies dormant within the formula of a "One beyond Being"—it lies, in other words, in recognizing in the "One beyond Being" a *henology* beyond *ontology*.

The distinction between henology and ontology has been familiar in the study of later Platonists and Aristotelians since Etienne Gilson's *Being and Some Philosophers* (1949), but Gilson's manner of drawing the distinction, however, is in itself ontologizing, and hence presents a distorted image of henology. Gilson regards henology as arising "[b]ecause existence as such seemed inconceivable," so that "metaphysical reflection ... spontaneously conceived being as 'that which is', irrespective of the fact 'that it is'."[78] As a result, Gilson views henology as a failed philosophical project inasmuch as "where being is posited as existentially neutral, it cannot play the part of a first principle."[79] Gilson's misreading of the nature of the henological first principle can be seen from his remark that "the One is nothing, because it is much too good to be something."[80] Gilson treats the henological first principle as though it is *a being* with strictures on its nomenclature, a misunderstanding facilitating the conflation of ancient Platonists and later proponents of "negative theology".

I wish to read Plato's doctrine in a manner much closer to that of Halper's Aristotle, for whom there is "a wedge between being and one"[81] since the three "primary ones"—that is, unity by continuity, by form and by formula—cannot be identified with one another, inasmuch as "it is possible for something to be a primary one in one way but not in the others."[82] For Aristotle this wedge has a structural form inasmuch as being is a *pros hen* or focal (hierarchized) manifold and unity is not. The

---

77 Couloubaritsis 2004: 383.
78 E. Gilson, *Being and Some Philosophers*, 2d ed. (Toronto: Pontifical Institute of Mediaeval Studies, 1952): 39.
79 Gilson 1952: 28.
80 Gilson 1952: 22.
81 Halper 2009: 129.
82 Halper 2009: 125.

significance of this reading of Aristotle for the doctrine of the "One beyond Being", once the latter has been freed from reification, is all the more remarkable in that Halper himself does not in the least hear the echoes of a Platonic discourse on 'the One' in a passage such as the following, in which he characterize's Aristotle's treatment of 'one': "there is no thing whose essence, as a thing, is to be one, no thing that is one itself … The essence of one, and all of its various determinations, are functions that real essences might have, but they are not themselves real essences."[83]

What I am calling henology is that part of metaphysics that, as Halper puts it, has no "intelligible content" because "the common character that makes all beings intelligible … is not itself intelligible as a character."[84] Indeed, the great virtue in Halper's henological Aristotle is that Halper feels not the least temptation to see in this a doctrine about something "much too good to be something." Accordingly, Halper distinguishes Aristotle's "primary one" from "a Platonic or Parmenidean one itself"[85] without argument—indeed, reflexively—as a result of a quite understandable reliance upon the dominant modern interpretation of Plato's henology as a doctrine concerning such an entity.

For this reason, the effort to understand Plato's henology receives the most direct assistance from authors who never speak of a "One beyond Being" and are thus free from the "danger" of which Couloubaritsis speaks. Thus McCabe argues in *Plato's Individuals* that the problem of individuation is the central and abiding concern in Plato's metaphysics, resulting in an account of individuation alternative to Aristotelian sortal individuation. McCabe has no cause to speak of 'the One' in a fashion pregnant with echoes of Gilsonian henology; rather, she *does* henology. With the help of such readings, it is possible to begin to elaborate a positive account of henology as a method for metaphysics, thereby transforming our understanding of Plato's legacy.

Verity Harte in *Plato on Parts and Wholes* sees the later Plato as increasingly concerned with *structure*. Structure is to henology,

---

83 Halper 2009: 143.
84 Halper 2009: xxxvii.
85 Halper 2009: 368.

we might say, what definition is to ontology. There are no privileged essential determinations of henological units; the injunction to "carve" reality "at the joints" (*Phaidr.* 265e) is manifestly quite a different matter.[86] Hence it is a mistake to see recourse to essential properties at *Phaid.* 102bc, when the point being made about 'inessential' properties in this passage is that they may be taken to belong to *another unity* according to their causality. Once Socrates has determined that, e.g., Simmias' tallness does not come about from the *causality* of Simmias, he proceeds to consider tallness in its own proper unity/agency, which is manifest in its causing things to be tall and never causing things to be short. This correlation between unity and causality/agency is a theme to which this essay shall return, as it is basic to Plato's thought, present in the way he formulates the very principle of noncontradiction (*Rep.* 436bc). Causality is at once 'in' structure and apart from it, structuring; and the problem of a relationship between structure and its exterior(s) creates a bridge between (1) *cause* in the *Philebus* which stands apart from the triumvirate of Limit, which "captures structures," the Unlimited, which is "the content in which such structure is found," and Mixtures, which are "contentful structures", in Harte's terms;[87] (2) the 'One' of the hypotheses of the *Parmenides*, the locus for the later Platonic tradition's understanding of henology; and (3) the *Republic*'s Good beyond Being.

The question of what Simmias is *qua* Simmias, and what is such a thing as to cause something to be Simmias and only Simmias, turns the debate about the soul and mortality in the *Phaedo* into a question of individuation. On the one hand, this gives it tractability. There is a special significance for henology of the particular problem at hand in the *Phaedo*, however, for what would be 'essential' to Simmias in this respect is not being 'a man'; it is being *Simmias* that is 'essential' to Simmias, and this is a question of certain unities that are in a privileged position, whether we consider them as structured or as structuring,

---

86 Cf. Cristina Ionescu's characterization of "the dialectician's mission" as "to keep applying the method until he reaches the ultimate metaphysical assumptions that validate a classification," ("The Unity of the *Philebus*: Metaphysical Assumptions of the Good Human Life," *Ancient Philosophy* 27 (2007), 55-75: 73).
87 Harte 2002: 189.

whether we take the question, that is, as 'What is Simmias?' or as '*Who* is Simmias?'. As McCabe puts it,

> Plato and Protagoras do perhaps have
> something in common. Protagoras's measure
> doctrine … is indifferent to who does the
> measuring; it may be a man or a god, a pig or
> a baboon … Being a measure is about being a
> person, not about being a member of a
> particular natural kind. The important thing,
> on that view, is to understand the special
> capacities of persons … that distinguish them
> from individual objects; and not to sort them
> into 'god-persons', 'parrot-persons', or even
> 'mechanical-persons'. The notion of being a
> person, on that account, takes priority over
> the natural kind to which the person belongs.
> The question is, "Who am I?"[88]

Shifting from the 'what' question to the 'who' question pivots the inquiry *within henology* from structured unity to the structuring (or measuring) agent unity. We must distinguish here what henology has to offer purely on account of the diversity of approaches or 'practices' available to it—for to approach an adequate determination of an individual *qua* individual requires the full resources of structural analysis, which includes structures that are internal (parts), external (relations), or temporal (narrative)—from the structured account of the cosmos, the ontology, that can be derived from the analysis of different modes of unity and the relations of implication among them.

McCabe remarks that "what Plato offers us is an analysis of individuation; let ontology wait until that is complete,"[89] and this restraint is crucial for us, inasmuch as we have largely lost sight of the methodological significance of henology altogether *and*, chiefly on account of this, misinterpreted whatever ontological results it offers. That it does indeed offer them is not in question even for McCabe, however, who shows how the "logic of consistency" in Plato's account of knowledge, which is

---

88 McCabe 1999: 279.
89 McCabe 1999: 257.

fundamentally henological, serves to develop "an argument for the nature of the thinking soul," such that "consistency has a great deal to do with persons," that is, with the particular mode of unity they exhibit.[90] In drawing such conclusions, however, we must never place the results over the method, for instance by grounding the method in a "One beyond Being", lest we lose the methodological thread once more. On the contrary, the present reading insists on interpreting all propositions of henology in terms of what *mode or modes of unity* they posit or explicate.

Inseparable from this henology is a science of structure that, I would argue, is Plato's 'arithmetic' proper, rather than any adoption of the methods or results of arithmetic in the narrow sense. Even before taking up the Platonic doctrine of 'ideal numbers', and whether they are 'numbers' in the familiar sense at all, the fact remains that a generalized *theory of multiplicities* is legitimately 'arithmetic', and the wish to pursue such a theory could be the basis for Plato's critique of mathematics narrowly understood as merely quantitative (*Phil.* 56de) or hypothetical (*Rep.* 533bc). Such a theory of manifolds does not deal with indifferent units, like the mathematics criticized in the *Philebus*, because different sorts of units differ precisely in the different sorts of multiplicities they form and that form them. Nor is it hypothetical, like the mathematics of the *Republic*, because whereas the geometry Plato has in mind there is dependent upon a particular and prior "dream about Being", henology, as Couloubaritsis has remarked, in virtue of its very principles, can aspire to discover new structures in advance of their worldly instantiation: "Je veux dire ... qu'en vertu des principes mêmes de l'hénologie, les possibilités des rapports entre tout et parties sont fort nombreuses et que l'on peut espérer en découvrir de nouvelles."[91] Similarly, Harte takes the object of the divine method in the *Philebus* to be "the constitution of the kind of

---

90 McCabe 1999: 285ff.

91 Couloubaritsis 2004: 414. One might compare the theory of manifolds in Husserl, by which, as Nikolay Milkov remarks, "we can construct an infinite number of forms of possible disciplines," for indeed, "any manifold can be seen as the form of a possible world" ("The Formal Theory of Everything: Explorations of Husserl's Theory of Manifolds," *Analecta Husserliana* 88 (2005), 119-35: 121, 127).

complex wholes that science studies; that is ... the constitution of entire scientific domains."[92] The geometer's 'dream' may be compared to Socrates' 'dream' in the *Theaetetus*, perhaps the paradigmatic dream for Plato, in that it proleptically reveals a domain of 'elements' (*stoicheia*) awaiting interpretation or appropriation.[93]

The science of structure, however, has immanent reference wherever it operates to a mode of unity beyond given determinations, a unity that is *structuring* rather than *structured*. As McCabe remarks, "the bundle argument," viz., "how is a collection *unified* when its unity can only be a member of the collection," is "a trap that will continue to threaten Plato's ontology until he can show that the organizing principle might not be one of the ordered items themselves,"[94] though this is not a trap, in my view, but rather a productive impasse, inasmuch as this problem leads ultimately to the proper conception of 'the One' to ground henology.

As Halper remarks, a "primary one", such as he thinks Plato affirms, "does not make something that belongs to it one; it makes the complex of itself and the other thing a plurality or, to the extent the other has no existence apart from a primary one, it makes the other less than one."[95] This is, however, a perfectly Platonic argument for why the One neither is, nor is one (*Parm.* 141e), for it is not *a* unit but *any* unit—cf. Halper's own argument that for Aristotle, "the one", "the primary one", "being *qua* being" and "one *qua* one" all refer to the nature of *any* being.[96] The identity of 'the One' in the ultimate sense is like the structural "zero symbolic value" of Lévi-Strauss, which if it expresses anything *for itself*, expresses the purely diacritical determination of the elements of the system. Note, in this respect, the acknowledgement at *Phil.* 23d that *diakrisis* may need to be introduced as a fifth element of being—the element, we might posit, permitting us to discriminate agency from mixtures.

---

92 Harte 2002: 199.
93 Cf. the remarks of Mitchell Miller in "Unity and Logos: A Reading of *Theaetetus* 201c-210a," *Ancient Philosophy* 12 (1992), 87-111, especially p. 104 n. 29.
94 McCabe 1999: 159.
95 Halper 2009: 367.
96 Halper 2009: 386f.

This discrimination is always deployed in some particular field, however. In the problem of the unity of the person, for example, the refusal to finally identify the self with any structured unity drives the inquiry in the *Phaedo* and reemerges in the Platonic doctrine of metempsychosis, which utterly sacrifices the identification of the self as *chooser* of a life with any stable features of that life: "But the *taxis* of the soul was not there [among the *paradeigmata*], because from the choice of a different life inevitably a different *<taxis>* comes to be [*gignesthai*]" (*Rep.* 618b), this choice belonging thus to the "family of the cause" from which come both mind and soul (*Phil.* 30b), i.e., as structured rather than structuring unities.[97]

It is possible to assign a hierarchical relationship to different modes of unity, and on a henological basis to determine a *prime* mode of unity as such, but there is nothing in such a notion that speaks to *how many* units there are exhibiting a given mode of unity, and ontology, for its part, will only determine *classes* of units. In this regard we must extend to the understanding of Plato's 'One' the Copernican shift which Alexander Mourelatos, and more recently Patricia Curd, have brought to the understanding of Parmenidean monism. According to Curd, Parmenides' doctrine is not *numerical monism*, which "asserts that there exists only one thing," so that "a complete list of entities in the universe would have only one entry," but rather *predicational monism*, which is "the claim that each thing that is can be only one thing ... a being of a single kind ... with a single account of what it is; but it need not be the case that there exists only one such thing."[98]

If there is a 'henological tendency' to be found in modern Plato scholarship, it would be said to have coalesced around the so-called 'anti-essentialist' themes, that is, those tending to undermine the centrality of a theory of forms in Plato. The present reading is 'anti-essentialist' as well inasmuch as it treats Plato's presumed ontological commitments as residua of diverse 'practices of unity' or methodological choices; but the 'anti-essentialists' are quite heterogeneous and in open conflict on

---

97 I have discussed this aspect of the problem further in "Animal and Paradigm in Plato," *Epoché* 18.2 (2014), 311-323.
98 P. Curd, *The Legacy of Parmenides: Eleatic Monism and Later Presocratic Thought* (Las Vegas: Parmenides Publishing, 2004): 5.

certain issues. On the one hand, there are those constituting
what Allan Silverman has labelled a new anti-essentialist
"orthodoxy", e.g. Fine, Annas, Moravcsik, McCabe et al.[99] Also
classifiable as 'anti-essentialist' is a growing body of scholarship
that displaces forms as such from a central place in Plato's
'ontology' in favor of unities such as souls and minds (see, e.g.,
Lloyd Gerson, *Knowing Persons*; Gerd van Riel, *Plato's Gods*). And
where in this picture ought one to place the so-called Tübingen
school, which displaces the theory of forms in the interest of a
doctrine of principles (*archai*) drawn from the testimonia and
careful reading of the dialogues?[100] Part of the purpose of the
present essay is to seek a harmony between these different
strains of 'anti-essentialism', a harmony made possible by the
ability to shift between methodological and ontological registers
within henology. Some anti-essentialists, such as Fine, suggest no
ontology for Plato. Indeed, it is precisely the treatment of
Platonic ontology by commentators that has frequently obscured
the very possibility of a discipline of henology by treating all of
the propositions of henology, in effect, as statements about
certain *entities*; herein lies the ambiguity for us in the status of
Plato's *archai*.

The mention of Tübingen raises the issue of so-called
unwritten doctrines in Plato. A point of value in the henological
reading I am proposing is that some of the confusion over the
'unwritten doctrines' in Plato can be seen as arising from the fact
that Aristotle presents Plato's methodology *ontologically*.
Aristotle's account from *Metaphysics* A6 uses the broad sense of
causality in Plato to treat an account of principles such as we
find in the *Philebus* as an ontology rather than, as we might
otherwise perceive it, a method for conceptual analysis whose
terms are analogical and trans-categorial unities, first among
which is the One itself. When Plato presents Limit and the
Unlimited as *elements* in the *Philebus*, he seems to invite the reader

---

99 A. J. Silverman, *The Dialectic of Essence: A Study of Plato's
Metaphysics*, (Princeton: Princeton University Press, 2002): 210,
352 n. 34.

100 For a useful overview, see especially Dmitri Nikulin's
introduction to D. Nikulin (ed.), *The Other Plato: The Tübingen
Interpretation of Plato's Inner-Academic Teachings* (Albany: SUNY
Press, 2012).

to treat his principles in just the sort of way that Aristotle does, as on a par with the *archai* of Presocratic natural philosophers, which for that matter were evidently in certain respects intended to function analogically as well. Elsewhere Aristotle seems to recognize the key terms in Plato's metaphysics as analogical unities. Thus Halper remarks on Aristotle's use of trans-categorial analogies "to consider together types of being that have no common character ... They [the analogies] function as classes beyond the highest genera."[101] Moreover, as the broadest *mode of unity* (*Met.* 1016b31-35), "analogy is intimately connected with the essence of one: one is a kind of analogy. As such, one is distinct from being," which is a *pros hen* or focalized/hierarchized manifold (Halper disputes Aquinas's identification of *pros hen* as a kind of analogy) and thus can be known and be the object of the science of metaphysics for Aristotle.[102]

Aristotle presents Plato's principles as yielding several levels of objects. The cause of "what something is" is the One and the forms, because anything is, first of all, one, and then some kind of one. The material cause within Aristotle's schema is Plato's "the Great and the Small". The *relative* nature of this principle, however, shows that it is hardly the same sort of 'matter' as, e.g., the bronze of the statue. Thus, as McCabe and Harte both argue, when Socrates illustrates the divine method in the *Philebus* using the examples of phonetics and music, limit is not to be taken as "actually 'applied' to something that might be described as undifferentiated sound ... implying the literal involvement ... of some 'sound stuff'."[103] For Harte, "[t]he unlimited components of a mixture ... do not constitute anything considered on their own";[104] rather, "[l]imit and unlimited are the twin ingredients in the *analysis* of mixtures ... not because members of each of these kinds are both parts of any mixture." Instead, members of the class of the unlimited are "parts ... conceived in the absence of structure," while "members of the class of limit are the structure of these parts, abstractly conceived."[105]

---

101 Halper 2009: 144.
102 Halper 2009: 145.
103 Harte 2002: 205 n. 79, with reference to McCabe 1999: 246.
104 Harte 2002: 194.
105 Harte 2002: 189.

Aristotle does not make the mistake of taking things like undifferentiated sound stuff as part of Plato's ontology in any absolute sense; nevertheless, Aristotle wishes to treat Plato's dyadic principle of "the Great and the Small" like the bronze in the statue when he states that numbers are produced from out of the Dyad "as if out of a moldable material" (988a1). Is the emphasis Aristotle gives to this portion of the doctrine perhaps to be explained in part by the fact that Plato has already taken his 'material' principle further from being concrete or plastic than the Pythagorean principle of a singular 'Unlimited' (987b26-7)? The innovation with respect to the Pythagoreans that Aristotle highlights here, that of taking the singular *apeiron* as a dyad, is in fact a decisive moment for henology as such, as I shall explain below, and this is acknowledged in the care Aristotle takes to mention what might seem a mere technicality. The interaction of the One and the dyad as the "causes of forms" and of forms and the dyad as "causes of sensibles", and the One and the dyad as causes of "good" and "ill" respectively, are likewise explicable through the relationship between *individuality* and *relative properties* in units, as I will also elaborate below.

Henology *can* yield ontological conclusions (e.g., the principle of non-contradiction as formulated at *Rep.* 436a & sq. is used to determine the unity and plurality of forms (*eidê*) in the soul according to their actions and passions), but these are contingent upon the outcome of an analysis of the sort of unity that different units possess—or that the same units possess under different henological 'practices'. In this way we can shed light on the problem of the possibility of "bad mixtures" in the *Philebus* account, and in general upon the Dyad as principle of evil for things. A mixture is "good" insofar as it is the product of an analysis adequate to some purpose. Other mixtures adjacent on the continuum are "bad" locally and relatively, i.e., to the degree that they do not represent a division "at the joints". On the plane of the cosmic individual, of which I will have more to say below, the total mixture is good; for units who form incompossible series, on the other hand, there are mixtures that are disintegrative or merely liminal for a certain unit, albeit they may be constitutive of some *other* unit on the same or a different scale. Here we recover the sense of the One as the cause of good for things and the Dyad as the cause of ill, for the One as a principle is constitutive of what is proper to some unit, while the

Dyad as a principle is constitutive of its *relativity*, and hence its tendency to be incorporated into some *other* unit.

The significance of Plato's 'Dyad' is thus, I believe, greatly obscured by taking it as a plastic substrate, and this systematic significance for henology is too important not to make an effort to free it altogether from this metaphoricity. A doctrine recorded most fully in Sextus Empiricus, but which echoes as well the report of Platonic doctrine attributed to Xenocrates and Hermodorus, posits a fundamental division of all things into *ta kath'heauta*, things that are in virtue of themselves, such as 'man' or 'horse', expressing the activity of the Monad, and *ta pros ti*, things that are relative to something, falling under the Dyad (*Adv. math.* 10.262-76; Diogenes Laertius III. 108f). On this understanding, the Dyad answers to just those properties the consideration of which has sometimes been taken as a prime motivation for the theory of forms itself. According to this thesis, there are forms originally and primarily of "incomplete properties", such as the virtues, about which there is often dispute, unlike properties such as 'human', 'fire', or 'water' (*Parm.* 130c) or 'bee' (*Men.* 72b). The method proposed in the *Philebus*, however, is considered broad enough to apply to "henads" such as 'human' and 'ox', which along with the Beautiful and the Good, are the subjects of the one/many disputes Socrates finds interesting in this dialogue. (The good, in the account from Sextus Empiricus, is regarded as not admitting of a difference of degree.) So the method of the *Philebus* can be applied, *mutatis mutandis*, alike to the "absolutes" and the "relatives" of the doxographers' reports.[106]

The Promethean method outlined is broad enough in its description to be able to encompass, in some fashion, both the "complete" and the "incomplete" properties, since it is

---

106 An interesting question, which I cannot take up here, concerns whether there is a particular significance to be attributed to the use of the term *henad* in the *Philebus* for units such as these, while the term *monad* is used for the results of "division". Fernando Muniz and George Rudebusch ("Plato, *Philebus* 15B: A Problem Solved," *Classical Quarterly* 54.2 (2004), 394-405) are, so far as I am aware, alone in having argued this, though it would foreshadow the technical usage these terms acquire in later Platonism.

expressed in terms broad enough to account for the full range of possible senses of "division" in these different cases. Later, the different products of the method, or its starting points, insofar as the method can be regarded as one of synthesis or analysis, will be distinguished, and the principles of a hierarchical disposition of things emerge, but in the first treatment of the method its virtue is its generality. The method, as presented there, is essentially the search for a discrete manifold or bounded multiplicity belonging to a chosen unit, in order to avoid the skeptical consequences of positing its undifferentiated unity or infinite multiplicity. Plato does not attempt at first to distinguish between dividing a unit in the sense of, e.g., distinguishing different varieties of oxen and in the sense of determining the organic parts into which an individual ox is divided. The Promethean method must belong to both if it is truly to be that by which all the accomplishments of the *technai* have been brought forth. The method thus can treat the unities called for in the *Parmenides* (135b-c), namely "a form under which each individual thing is classed," or in the *Republic* (596a), which posits forms "for each multiplicity to which we give the same name." But we should not assume that it does not operate quite differently in different cases.

Certain of the virtues, such as Beauty in the *Symposium*, or Justice, Temperance, or Knowledge in the *Phaedrus*, are subject to a kind of intuition; it seems doubtful that forms such as Greatness and Smallness would be. But perhaps the intuitability of the former is not incompatible with their being "woven together" as in the *Sophist*, and therefore susceptible to collection and division. McCabe has argued that we need not regard the vision of the Good in the *Republic* as that of a "single and simple item … grasped raw and unmediated."[107] I have argued elsewhere that the forms of the virtues subsist inseparably in the eternal persons of the Gods for Plato, if we take the account in the *Phaedrus* at face value; and I have argued that to do so is by no means as bad an option as it has seemingly been regarded.[108]

---

107 M. M. McCabe, "Is Dialectic as Dialectic Does? The Virtue of Philosophical Conversation," in *The Virtuous Life in Greek Ethics*, B. Reis and S. Haffmans (eds.) Cambridge: Cambridge University Press, 2006), 70-98: 93.
108 See my "Plato's Gods and the Way of Ideas," *Diotima: Review*

The terminology of "separation" with respect to such forms applies to their separation from *contingent*, as opposed to eternal and essential participants, while the terminology of "themselves by themselves" refers to their freedom from contamination by their opposites. Fine has argued against "separate" having the sense of "independent existence" in these contexts, and her arguments are only strengthened if the *mutual* separation between the realms of *genesis* and *ousia*[109] is in fact nothing other than the separation, relatively non-controversial in mainstream Hellenic belief, between the realm of mortals and the realm of the deathless Gods.[110]

The superior integrity of the divine individuals to embodied ones, which bears on the relationship such individuals have to form(s), is also a key element in Gerson's person-centered anti-essentialism. At *Charmides* 169a, Socrates remarks that a "great man" is needed to determine adequately "whether there is no being naturally having its own potency [*dunamis*] in relation to itself, or only in relation to another." In this process, the simple—or structuring—agent unity, the *cause* in the *Philebus*, partakes of relationality, the *pros ti*. An example of such a *dunamis* acting upon itself is, Gerson argues, the *sumphutos dunamis* of the soul (*Phaedrus* 246a6-7), operating through the *dunamis* of the understanding to differentiate itself into "really distinct but inseparable parts." Gerson notes that "the *Republic* does not specifically refer to the parts of the soul as *dunameis*; the regular word used is *eidos*. The virtues, however, are occasionally referred to as *dunameis*, and in *Republic* V *epistêmê* and *doxa* are distinct *dunameis*, presumably of *to logistikon*."[111] There appears to be a

---

of Philosophical Research 39, 73-87. Van Riel's *Plato's Gods* (Farnham: Ashgate, 2013) goes a long way toward correcting the bias that has obscured the systematic importance of the Gods in Plato's thought.

109 G. Fine, *Plato on Knowledge and Forms* (Oxford: Oxford University Press, 2003): 274.

110 R. Bodéüs (*Aristotle and the Theology of the Living Immortals*, trans. Jan Garret (Albany: SUNY Press, 2000)) has discussed the importance for Aristotle of notions drawn from traditional Greek theology, and as Van Riel points out, the situation is not so different for Plato as Bodéüs suggests.

111 L. P. Gerson, "A Note on Tripartition and Immortality in

continuum of differentiation relative to an integral unit, in which the mediating position is occupied by *dunameis* that are fluid with respect to number and division, with forms being the ultimate products of such a process of hypostatization. Hence we can adopt different perspectives on the same units, on the one hand intuitable in themselves, on the other "woven together". Socrates is not being coy when he defers to a "great man" to resolve the question of identity here, whether something may act upon itself *as such* and not *qua* other, for this problem leads directly to the heart of henology and hence to the *Parmenides*, and to the "great man" Parmenides himself.

The virtues are ultimately, Plato explains in the *Republic*, to be related to the form of the Good according to a "longer way" than that inquiry which yielded provisional accounts of them from the tripartite structure of the soul (*Rep.* 435d, 504ab). The form of the Good suggests a teleological structure of the cosmos; but how to take the first step on the "longer way"? We would have a start if this teleological structure itself *explicates the nature of individuality*. In this respect, the form of the Good would necessarily be something more than "the system of forms suitably interrelated," as Fine proposes.[112] We know that by virtue of it the genuine dialectician is able to give an account of the being of *each thing* (*hekaston*, *Rep.* 534b). Individuality can supply a bond between the greatest individual, the cosmos, and the least, the individual particular. Plato is not a foundationalist; but as Fine acknowledges in her basically coherentist reading, coherence is not sufficient for knowledge, "but only for justification; knowledge also requires truth."[113] Hence there is an ineliminable role for perception, which McCabe argues is not for Plato "raw or unmediated," but "does still have a peculiar feature of veridicality," which has to do with its *unity*: "perception makes its reports wholesale."[114] Truth is also, along with beauty and proportion, the "dwelling" of the Good, according to the *Philebus* (64c), the primitives, so to speak, of the system.

Not all 'forms' are alike in this regard. The virtues adduced in the *Phaedrus*, and above all the trio of Beauty, Truth and

---

Plato," *Apeiron* 20 (1987), 81-96: 91.
112 Fine 2003: 396.
113 Fine 2003: 111.
114 McCabe 2006: 94.

Proportion, play a privileged role with respect to the individual integrity of the most complex unities, namely souls and minds. In fact, they are only with difficulty to be distinguished from this very integrity. They are relative *in us*, to be sure, for even Helen is ugly relative to Aphrodite, but Aphrodite is not ugly in relation to anything (*Hipp. mai.* 289a sq.). But what of the forms to which relativity is integral?

Here the unusual theory of relations Plato adduces in the *Phaedo* becomes important. The key to this theory is that the single relation of, e.g., Simmias being taller than Socrates is broken up into the monadic qualities of Simmias's tallness and Socrates' shortness. This general approach to relations is also, I believe, expressed in Plato's reported replacement of the unitary Pythagorean principle of the Unlimited with a Dyadic principle of relativity. Treating their relations as monadic qualities has the effect of restoring to Simmias and Socrates a degree of individual integrity which they would lose to the unitary relation. On Hector-Neri Castañeda's reading,[115] it is the forms of Tall and Short, rather, which create a "form-chain" of reciprocal implication, and thus lose their autonomy: something's tallness requires something else's shortness. Simmias' tallness does not require Socrates' shortness, though; the demand arises from the determination's ideality. The relativity belongs to the form, rather than the individual.

The integrity purchased for individuals in this fashion does not, however, prevent them from suffering the compresence of opposites: Simmias has tallness relative to Socrates, but shortness relative to Phaedo. Traits like these render individuals discernible, like the distinctive assemblage of facial features that allow Socrates to recognize Theaetetus (*Theait.* 209b sq.). But is the individual nothing more than a bundle of such qualities? If we take Plato's affirmations of metempsychosis seriously, then the individual cannot be reducible to such qualities, because

---

115 See H. N. Castañeda, "Plato's *Phaedo* Theory of Relations," *Journal of Philosophical Logic* 1 (1972), 467-480; "Plato's Relations, Not Essences or Accidents at *Phaedo* 102b2-d2," *Canadian Journal of Philosophy* 8 (1978), 39-53; for broader implications, see Castañeda's "Leibniz and Plato's *Phaedo* Theory of Relations and Predication," in *Leibniz: Critical and Interpretive Essays*, M. Hooker (ed.) (Minneapolis: Minnesota University Press, 1982), 124-159.

none of them—not even humanity—necessarily accompany that individual into his/her next incarnation. This is, of course, to rest an important theoretical assertion upon an admittedly enigmatic doctrine. Leibniz's aporia concerning reincarnation could not entirely have escaped Plato; the identity of someone who shares no *determinate* qualities with me is utterly paradoxical. But then again, perhaps that is the point of the doctrine, that is, to indicate the nonidentity of the (structuring) individuator in the individual with any such (structured) quality.[116]

Plato never indicates that he wishes to identify anyone in particular from life to life. What he emphasizes, rather, are the consequences of individual *choices* for the integrity or disintegration of the self. That is, the use to which Plato mostly puts the doctrine of metempsychosis is that of *henological ethics*. Certain dispositions of the self disintegrate it by integrating it into systems inconsistent with identity as an individual agent. As McCabe remarks, Plato

> does have an account to give of the first person; but the context in which it is given pushes him toward the view that being a unified person is not something I can take for granted ... but rather something to which I aspire ... hence, the proper question to ask is indeed, Who shall I become? (ref. to *Protagoras* 311b).[117]

It does not seem that Plato believes in absolute annihilation for any soul, so the tendency toward disintegration has a limit: the agency of the self is *categorially*—not empirically— ineliminable even in this disintegrative activity. It is not a

---

116 In this respect Richard Sorabji is correct to underscore the significance of Porphyry's affirmation that the bundle of qualities constitutive of an individual "would not" belong to another, rather than the weaker affirmation in Boethius that it merely "will not" ("Porphyry on Self-Awareness, True Self, and Individual," in *Studies on Porphyry*, G. Karamanolis and A. Sheppard (eds.) (London: Institute of Classical Studies, 2007), 61-69: 67).
117 McCabe 1999: 264.

question of reidentifying selves, but of distinguishing structure and what structures in the self. We have a bias toward virtue inasmuch as virtue is consistent with the agency which is the vital thread of the self. Similarly, we tend toward true beliefs because our own unity is consistent with the unity, or intelligibility, of all that we might come to know. The epistemological relevance of the doctrine of recollection in the *Meno* has nothing to do with any of the particularities of an individual's prior lives, but with the notion of an unrestricted intelligibility of the universe in which there are no fundamental incompatibilities that would, so to speak, regionalize intelligence; and this epistemic universality also extends the horizon of the question "Who shall I become?" to the worlds—contiguous individuals or singularities—composible with the individual I thus become.

The question of the universality of intelligence brings us to the cosmic individual of the *Timaeus* and the support it renders for the holistic epistemology which has been associated with the so-called anti-essentialist position as present in, e.g., Fine, though not those such as Gerson or, more questionably, the Tübingen reading. One aspect of the henological reading would seem to rest uneasily with holism: it is generally assumed that the latter has eliminated any significant role for intuition in Plato's later thought. But if intuition were vital for securing the forms as discrete entities,[118] then would it not be just as vital for a theory in which individuality is primitive?

As I have indicated, however, what is from one point of view the unitary object of an intuition may be compound from another point of view. Even if these 'points of view' be taken as ontologically productive, nothing requires that the positions of unit and composite be occupied by all and only the same items at all times. The description of the Promethean method in the *Philebus* implies that the same units could be divided in different ways. Justice in the *Republic* consists in harmonizing the three principles in the soul, marked out in purely relative terms as lowest, highest and mean, "and all others there may happen to be in between" (443de). The *Timaeus* presents the forms, treated in other works as distinct, as inhering in the Living Thing Itself

---

118 See, for instance, Silverman's appeal to the *Seventh Letter* (Silverman 2002: 216, 353 n. 42).

or *Autozóion*. The virtues are treated as one at one time but at another distinguished in accord with the distinction of the powers in the soul; it has been suggested that the virtues exhibit a formal structure in which the particular virtues are at once parts of virtue as a whole, but also each *identical* to virtue as a whole.[119]

Differences such as these regarding the forms and the virtues are usually taken as signs of changes in Plato's thinking on these matters. A middle ground is offered by McCabe, who sees a dialectic of "austere" and "generous" ways of conceiving the individuals in question in particular dialogues as driving Plato's philosophical progress. Here, then, there is both development *and* a unitary method. But I will go further than McCabe in claiming that "austere" and "generous" individuation represents more than an ongoing problematic in Plato; it is also a *result*. The *Timaeus* is particularly salient in this respect.

The *Timaeus* attempts to situate the forms in a more comprehensive ontological framework by relating their mode of unity to that of the soul and the latter to the unity of the *animal as such* and to the cosmos. The soul's elements in the *Timaeus* are Sameness and Difference in two different respects, namely divisible and indivisible; we can take the mixture of divisible and indivisible Being as the "contentful structure" from which, for Harte, the former are analytically derived. Analyzing the sameness and difference in the soul in the manner one would analyze Sameness and Difference according to the 'practice' of the first hypothesis of the *Parmenides*, the practice of 'austere' individuation, as it were, one would find that sameness is in no way different and difference is in no way the same, and both would thus be paradoxical units; according to the 'generous' individuation of the second hypothesis, however, sameness is also different and difference is also the same. This is, of course, the perspective taken up by the Eleatic stranger in the *Sophist*, in which we find that forms such as sameness and difference are in fact "interwoven" with one another. With its "indivisible" and "divisible" sameness and difference, however, the *Timaeus* psychogony goes a step further, making the soul the locus for structure, with one foot in the *Parmenides'* first hypothesis and

---

119 See M. T. Ferejohn, "Socratic Virtue as the Parts of Itself," *Philosophy and Phenomenological Research* 44.3 (1984), 377-388.

one in the second: at once a (structuring) unit virtually ineffable in its self-identity and a Heraclitean contradictory whole,[120] mediated by a determinate manifold or bounded multiplicity of differentiated (structured) 'parts' or faculties. In this way, the soul is the primary site for supra-mathematical 'arithmetic'.

The paradigmatic function of the forms in the *Timaeus* rests in the proposition that the cosmos is ordered by the demiurge in a relationship of resemblance to the animal or living thing itself, that is, the living thing *qua* living. Plato's ambiguity with respect to the identity of the living thing in question has led scholars such as Gerson to argue, with good reason, that the demiurge and the paradigm ought to be regarded as actually identical.[121] But does Plato wish us to understand some particular living being at all, or is the point rather that the demiurge has fashioned the cosmos according to the properties of an eternal living being as such, properties which are present immediately for the demiurge by analyzing himself, or any other of the Gods? I have argued elsewhere that the vision of the forms in the *Phaedrus* presupposes that they are 'seen' *in* the Gods themselves, and that divine beauty in particular is to the virtue-forms what, e.g., fire is to the form of the hot in the *Phaedo*.[122] But beyond this, if what matters are the properties, rather than the identity, it would then be as much of a mistake to ask *which* living thing the demiurge has used as a model, as it would be to take Aristotle's remark that 'the One' is a substance for Plato as referring to a certain singular substance.

Timaeus' account that the cosmos—the order in things— comes about in and through a relationship of likeness to *that*

---

120 McCabe notes the "Heraclitean tone" Socrates adopts at *Charmides* 166d, that he might fail to "track himself down," ("Looking Inside Charmides' Cloak: Seeing Others and Oneself in Plato's Charmides," in *Maieusis: Essays on Ancient Philosophy in honor of Myles Burnyeat*, D. Scott (ed.) Oxford: Oxford University Press, 2007), 1-19: 18).

121 L. P. Gerson, *Knowing Persons: A Study in Plato* (Oxford: Oxford University Press, 2006): 249f; see previously E. Perl, "The Demiurge and the Forms: A Return to the Ancient Interpretation of Plato's *Timaeus*," *Ancient Philosophy* 18 (1998), 81-92.

122 "Plato's Gods and the Way of Ideas," op cit.

which lives, insofar as it lives explains how the cosmos offers itself as intelligible to the living, namely according to the principle that 'like knows like', and that the forms are not to be conceived apart from the *analysis of the cosmos into its animals, and the self-analysis of those animals*. It is not the living thing *qua* part of the whole which serves as the cosmic paradigm, but the living thing as incorporating the totality: "All nature is akin, and the soul has learned everything" (*Men.* 81d). The living thing is the paradigm of the cosmos only when understood in this fashion, namely as encompassing all that truly is. This is not the prerogative solely of some exotic being, but rather the nature of every individual when the holistic conditions of its determination are accepted. (Note, in this respect, that the same term, *paradeigma*, is used in the *Republic*'s Myth of Er to refer to the life-pattern each soul chooses, which must incorporate a compossible world-series.)

The first two hypotheses of the *Parmenides* ground two basic henological 'practices'. The first hypothesis recognizes *every* individual as unique in every respect—albeit from the perspective of ontology such an individual is, literally, *nothing*, its integrity transcending even unity and being inasmuch as the latter belong to a structured rather than a structuring unity—while the second hypothesis affirms for each individual the principle *panta en pasin*. Neither is intended to be eliminated, nor is either correctly understood as identifying some *particular* entity, rather than a way of conceiving *any* individual. These two 'practices' gain determinacy through the *Timaeus* psychogony.

In the *Timaeus*, as McCabe notes, we have an "account of the constitution of the identity of the world <which> may be understood as quite general, a view of the identity of any thing we care to think about."[123] This account offers "two different perspectives for individuation—one internal and absolute, the other external and context-relative," corresponding to "a contrast between deciding the internal *unity* of something and counting it as a *unit* by determining its identity vis-à-vis other individuals." But "questions about internal unity and questions about identity in context are complementary," for the individual "understood as merely contextual" is "characteristically austere—they have no features in and of themselves (at least so long as the relations in which they stand are thought of as

---

123 McCabe 1999: 169.

features of the relata ...)," whereas "if we focus upon the internal constitution of some 'one', then we may allow it to have parts; at that stage we need to supply some cohesive principle to hold the parts together and to individuate the whole," i.e., the individual is "generous".[124] The contextually-individuated unit thus turns out to be *atomic*, and can be *unique* insofar as its contextual manifold is purely negative, as in the case of the cosmos, for which "by exhausting the 'without', unity is ensured,"[125] or as in Damascius' argument, at the culmination of antique Platonic thought, for the absolute negativity of the first principle, which depends upon the integrity of totality *stricto sensu* (*panta haplôs*)[126]—while the internally-individuated unit turns out to have so many internalized relations as to render it a virtual universe.

Although it was not indicated in the *Parmenides* that the first two hypotheses were complementary, in the *Timaeus* it is clear that the cosmic individual is successfully individuated *both* absolutely and contextually. That is, it is a unity from within, by virtue of its internal order (*Tim.* 31b-32c) and from without, because it exhausts the available material (33a).[127] In this regard, the argument for the unity of the cosmos is transformed into an argument for the *uniqueness* of any putative individual. The crux of the henological reading of the *Timaeus* thus lies in the sense of the word *monogenês*, namely whether it is to be understood as "only begotten" or "single-in-genus", the same dispute which has arisen over Parmenides' use of the term in frag. B8.4, the latter reading being central to Curd's argument that Parmenides' monism is "predicational" rather than "numerical".[128] The two senses can be brought into alignment in discussing the cosmic individual, which is a good reason for individuation to, as it were, take a cosmological detour. But every animal, that is, every living thing and, mediately, every object of animal intelligence insofar as it is dependent upon the unity of that animal— compare the use of animals (*zôia*) as the paradigmatic "absolutes" (*kath'heauta*) for Plato according to Diogenes

---

124 McCabe 1999: 167.
125 McCabe 1999: 166.
126 See my "Damascian Negativity" (*Dionysius*, forthcoming).
127 McCabe 1999: 165f.
128 On which see Curd 2004: 71-3.

Laertius (III. 108f)—is the beneficiary of the criteria established for the cosmic animal, criteria according to which its primary unity is not that of a member of a species, but an "only begotten", one-of-a-kind individual. Compare the argument at *Theaet.* 209a that knowledge of something cannot be of what it has in common with other things; knowledge of Simmias *qua* 'human' therefore cannot be knowledge of Simmias, but of the human form, and animality in the 'paradigmatic' Timaean sense is thus superior to 'humanity' in the narrow sense.

In the two individuating practices demonstrated in the *Timaeus* with respect to the exemplary or paradigmatic cosmic individual, no account is taken of the possible different ways in which the structure of the individual may be expressed. There can be no question of taking the cosmic individual in the light of different relations, of course, because the cosmic individual has no exterior; it is a windowless monad. But that does not mean that there is not relativity. In the *Timaeus*, this is only implicit in the emphasis upon the demiurge's discrete act of ordering the cosmos according to the living paradigm; any such discrete act implies different possible schematisms. But the *Theaetetus* raises the issue regarding a "totality" (*pan*) such as the number 6, which, although it is not a Timaean 'universe', has in common with the latter that it *lacks* nothing (205a). Socrates points out that there are a number of *wholes* pertaining to such a totality. Six can be enumerated by counting to six, or as twice three, or thrice two, or by various acts of addition (204bc). These are, as Socrates puts it, the plural totalities (*ta panta*) complementary to the singular totality (*to pan*) of the Six.

A fortiori a Speusippean individual, which is in the absolute sense like a dimensionless point representing the nexus or center of a universe whose sole purpose is to constitute this individual, is for any given purpose constituted instead as a *circle* of some definite dimension. This is necessary if we acknowledge that according to all the evidence Speusippus was not a skeptic on account of his holism. Numbers such as six are for Speusippus paradigmatic of direct knowledge, and yet he recognizes their parts and their relations. Tarán points to this as "a difficulty in Speusippus' conception of numbers and magnitudes because, on the one hand, they have to function as individual entities which are the objects of knowledge, while, on the other hand, they ought to be nothing but relations."[129] But this is not perhaps a difficulty at all. Numbers, and after them, geometrical magnitudes, are paradigmatic intelligibles precisely because it is easier in their case than in the case of other things for us to grasp this essential complementarity, which only becomes more paradoxical to grasp in the more complex entities in which, nevertheless, Speusippus insisted the Good resides. And as Plato has Timaeus assert, it is "always said" that what is fair and good is *constructed* (*xunistanai*) out of things that are not such in and of themselves (*Tim.* 53b). "Always said" here finds an echo in Aristotle's comparison of Speusippus' doctrine to that of the "theologians ... who say ... that the good and the noble appeared after the nature of things progressed" (*Met.* 1091a34), and so it is fitting that Plato inserts it into his "theological" account, that is, an account which resembles that of the ancient theologians in giving pride of place to intelligent agents, living things, rather than the mechanical forces of the naturalists.

To the degree that something has what we might term an organic unity, a "nature" (*Theait.* 174a), this nature "prescinds from the whole-part structure it calls for and is, by contrast with the thing which has this structure, simple. But at the same time ... the 'nature' expresses itself in the medium of the things that have it ... In this indirect way, in the organization it exacts of others, the 'nature' is subject to whole-part analysis,"[130] an analysis which involves recognizing "its kinship, through shared intermediate level parts, with other things."[131] There is thus no hard and fast distinction between analyzing something into its parts and incorporating it into a schema of collection and division.

But what of the unitary 'nature', which is obliquely posited again at *Sophist* 255e: "each thing is not different [*heteron*] from the others through its own nature, but through participating in the idea of the Different"? The nature which 'prescinds' in this way from the structure it deploys does so, not as a matter of simple abstraction, save perhaps in the limit case, but just insofar as it exercises the appropriate structuring *agency*. Unity of this primary mode is the unity of a cause, agent unity. This is already apparent in the *Phaedo*, whose final argument turns ultimately not

---

129 L. Tarán, *Speusippus of Athens* (Leiden: E. J. Brill, 1981): 59.
130 Miller 1992: 98.
131 Miller 1992: 99.

on forms, but on form *bringers* such as fire or a soul. The pinnacle of the *aporiai* concerning the forms in the introductory section of the *Parmenides* comes when it seems that the doctrine of the forms will make it impossible for the Gods, who are the cosmic agents *par excellence*, to exercise any agency. It is this realization which, above all, requires that the theory of forms be transcended in some fashion, though not abandoned, lest the power of discourse be destroyed (*Parm.* 135c). The primacy of *unity* in this way serves to preserve the primacy of *practice*.

The present essay has offered a conception of Platonic talk about 'the One' for which the latter simply *is* the diverse henological practices or modes of analysis of unity or individuation presented in the several hypotheses of the *Parmenides* and which can also be understood as applications of the Promethean method from the *Philebus*. Taken together, these constitute the foundation of what we may regard as a Platonic structuralism. I have sought to distinguish henology in this productive sense from its products, whether those belonging to the *technai* which are philosophy's siblings, so to speak, relative to the Promethean method, or those belonging to philosophy, and which it is convenient to term ontology. There is, to be sure, a broad sense of ontology which would be virtually coextensive with henology; however, insofar as ontology has become almost synonymous with an effort to *narrow* the scope of being and to establish a hierarchy of objects and methods of inquiry, it is necessary to differentiate henology, in the sense of the present essay, from ontology in this familiar sense more strictly. I believe that the flexibility of henology as I have attempted to present it, with the capacity to operate across diverse and otherwise incommensurable ontologies in the narrow sense, recommends it as a subject for further exploration beyond the strictly Platonic context; but there is surely value in recognizing in any such appropriation a genuine continuity with the Platonic tradition.

100

On the Gods and the Good[*]

> Each of us is one, but that very thing which
> *each* of us is, *both* of us are not; for we are not
> one but *two*.
> — Plato, *Hippias Major* 301d

> Don't you think it is the *common* good of
> everybody, more or less, for it to become
> evident how it is with *each* being?
> — Plato, *Charmides* 166d

Near the end of a long career in which he had articulated his
philosophical doctrines indirectly in the form of dialogues, and
in private to a circle of students, Plato decided to make a direct,
public statement in the form of a lecture that is known as *On the
Good*. Unfortunately, it does not survive; we know its contents
primarily from a memorable account deriving ultimately from
Plato's student Aristotle, who attended the lecture. Aristotle's
brief account dwells on the lecture's reception, which was not
positive. It was not that there was anything distasteful in Plato's
lecture; rather, it seems merely that it was very technical and
confusing, and failed to speak directly to the issues his audience
expected to hear about in a lecture on the Good. In particular,

---

* Lecture presented at the Polytheist Leadership Conference,
Fishkill, NY, July 12, 2014.

we are told that his extensive recourse to mathematics, and his final conclusion, that the Good is the One, or Unity, left his audience perplexed and, probably, bored.

There are certain aspects of this account which ought to cause us, before even attempting to reconstruct from Plato's surviving works what he might have been saying, to question some assumptions so widespread in modern commentators as to go virtually unremarked upon and, certainly, unquestioned. These assumptions concern what in general Plato meant by 'the One'. They are so widespread and unquestioned because they accord with the appropriation of Platonic thought by Christian monotheism, an appropriation which was by no means peaceful in antiquity. This struggle, however, is treated as a footnote in the history of philosophy, to the extent that the waning of Christian hegemony in the intellectual life of the West has led to no wholesale reconsideration of received notions about the sense and import of classical metaphysics. Modern thinkers, while distancing themselves from the monotheistic project *per se*, have nevertheless treated that project's conception of the goals and sense of Hellenic philosophy as though it was more or less *correct*.

According to this view, when Plato spoke of the One, or of the Good, he was speaking of a *singular item*, either a singular item beyond everything, or a singular item encompassing everything. Scholars will plead that their interpretations are far more subtle and complex than this, but a radical *alternative* reading can, I believe, show just how profound is the distortion in our received understanding of the tradition of classical metaphysics. It is a simple matter to catalogue affirmations of polytheistic devotion in Plato's works, and scholars have at last begun to offer unbiased accounts of Plato's theology from the things he explicitly says about the Gods, rather than fabricating a theology for him conforming to modern prejudices.[132] What remains, however, is to address the obfuscation crucial to the entire project of the monotheistic appropriation of classical metaphysics, namely *the meaning and significance of 'one' (τὸ ἓν) in Greek philosophy*.

---

132 See, notably, Gerd Van Riel, *Plato's Gods* (Farnham, Surrey: Ashgate, 2013).

The necessity for such clarification arises immediately from the language itself. Like any similar expression in Greek composed of the neuter definite article in front of an adjective or participle—such as *to ison*, 'the equal', *to kalon*, 'the beautiful'—*to hen* is ambiguous. Such terms can refer to a particular thing exhibiting a certain property, as long as the gender is appropriate, or to everything that exhibits that property, or to the property itself, what we would usually designate by a term like 'unity', 'equality' or 'beauty'. This abstract aspect can be underscored by adding the term *auto*, 'itself', though it does not require it. It is in the nature of Greek to be able to form such expressions at will, and Greek philosophy takes every advantage of this. This ambiguity is not limited to terms with the neuter article, either. To use one notorious example, *ho theos*, 'the God', refers ambiguously to a particular God indicated in the context, or as a means to talk about things true of Gods in general, in which case it is freely interchangeable with *hoi theoi*, 'the Gods'. A philosophical inquiry into *to hen* or *auto to hen*, therefore, is most naturally understood as an inquiry into *the nature of unity*, what it is for something to be *one* thing or one *something*.

In philosophy, one hears of "the problem of the one and the many", referring to an entire genre of inquiry already well known by Plato's time. In fact, Plato is already keen to distinguish serious or interesting problems of this kind from vapid ones. Thus, in the *Philebus*, Socrates speaks of certain one-and-many problems as "childish", "glib", and "a hindrance to discussion" (*Philebus* 14d-e).[133] In the *Sophist*, too, Plato speaks of "youngsters and elders whose learning has come to them late in life," who "feast" upon trivial one-and-many problems (*Sophist* 251a-c). These specious treatments of the one and the many have as their common end, Plato says, that "the one is many and infinite and the many only one" (*Philebus* 14e) or that "each thing we posit as one we in turn treat as many and call by many names" (*Sophist* 251b). We see, therefore, that Plato is well aware of a tendency for one-and-many problems to be treated in an unserious way, a degree of critical insight that speaks to a development and refinement of the terms of this discussion over a period of time.

---

133 All translations from the *Philebus* and from the *Sophist* are by H. N. Fowler, occasionally modified.

What, then, does Plato regard as a serious and worthy discussion to have about one and many? In the *Philebus*, Socrates explains that the interesting discussions come with respect to unities like "the Human", meaning not this particular human, but what we call the species; or "the Bovine"; or "Beauty"; or, indeed, "the Good" (15a). Plato makes clear in this way that he is interested in unities, 'ones', that lack a simple, unproblematic basis. The examples he offers proceed from the less problematic to those more so. Natural kinds like humans and oxen surely have something real to them; they reproduce themselves continuously and always show some common traits, amid much variation as well. A unit such as Beauty is more contested. It holds together sufficiently as a concept for us to talk about it, at least, and understand one another, though we take for granted that *judgments* of beauty are highly subjective. Finally, there is the Good—and we know to begin with that what is good for one thing is by no means good for another, so even if we might hope in the case of Beauty to arrive at canons of beauty, or, in a more sophisticated move, in rules for the judgment of beauty that allow for its subjectiveness, it's going to be rather more difficult to figure out how to conceive a unity such as the Good, assuming that it's really something more than just hot air.

Unities like these are problematic. At minimum, they pop up at different times and places, and with all sorts of variations that threaten their unity, while in cases like Beauty and Goodness their instances conflict directly with one another in non-trivial ways. But these problems clearly concern determinate unities and expect determinate answers, unlike the pseudo-problems of the "late learners" and their ilk. How are we to get a handle on serious one-and-many problems? Plato's answer in the *Philebus* is a method Socrates characterizes as both ancient and as "a gift from the Gods to humans" (16c, again at 16e), and which he says forms the basis of all arts and crafts. This method is based on the notion that "things ever said to exist are from One and Many, and have Limit and Unlimited inherent in them." The method operationalizes this fundamental insight about beings. It works like this:

> [W]e must always assume that there is in every case one idea concerning everything and must look for it—for we shall find that it is there—

> and if we get a grasp of this, we must look
> next for two, if there be two, and if not, for
> three or some other number; and again we
> must treat each of those units in the same
> way, until we can see not only that the original
> One is one and many and infinite, but just
> how many it is. And we must not apply the
> idea of the infinite to plurality until we have a
> view of the total number of it between infinity
> and one; then, and not before, we may let
> each One of all things pass on unhindered
> into infinity. (16de)

Let's review this procedure. We're curious about something; since we even have that much notion of it, we have some *One* to start with. Then we try to see if that one idea is somehow really two, or if not, three or some other number. It's not an additive process. Rather, the initial One is either going to stay one, or its going to yield some distinct number: if it's three, then it's *not* two, apparently. It seems a bit like searching for the number that will divide another without remainder. Then the units that come from this process each get analyzed in the same way. Each One is one, and it's also Many, that is, a discrete number, and it's infinite, in other words, a continuum. The initial unity of the unit and its infinity or continuity mirror each other at the beginning and end of the procedure, while in between we have a discrete multiplicity. And Plato is quite clear that what's wrong with the people drawn in by the spurious one-and-many problems is that *they aren't interested in discrete multiplicities*, rather, "they put infinity immediately after unity; they disregard all that lies between them," whereas it is a concern with *finite multiplicities* that distinguishes serious from vapid discussions (17a).

I'm not going to concern myself with the examples given in the *Philebus* of the method, things like finding the number of tones between two musical notes or devising an alphabet to represent the sounds of spoken language. Rather, I'd like to keep the focus on the most universal dimension of the method and think a little about what it means, all on its own, for the lecture on the Good. For one thing, we can see that any interpretation that would make Plato's meaning in equating the One and the Good be that *all things are one thing, and this is good* would fall right into the trap Plato sees having caught his contemporary "wise men", namely, becoming obsessed with the direct identity between the unity of the universe, on the one hand, and the infinity of things in the universe, on the other. Plato has thus, it would seem, already rejected a certain monism—and a corresponding monotheism—as at any rate not philosophically interesting, and so this interpretation of the meaning of the doctrine put forward in the lecture on the Good would seem to be ruled out at the start. In the method, 'One' is always *some one*, some one thing whose integrity or individuality we are testing, to see how it holds together, and what kind of discrete multiplicity or number (*arithmos*) can be elicited from it. This orientation is previewed early in the *Philebus* in an interesting fashion.

The *Philebus* begins from the question of what condition of the soul makes life happy. Protarchus, on behalf of Philebus, argues that it is pleasure; Socrates, that it is wisdom. Philebus, who leaves early, has made some sort of statement offstage, so to speak, concerning a Goddess. Socrates seizes upon this statement and says, "Let us begin with the very Goddess whom Philebus says is spoken of as Aphrodite but most truly named Pleasure [*Hêdonê*]" (12b). It is clear from what Socrates says that Philebus embellished his argument in favor of pleasure as the best disposition of the soul by stating that in upholding the primacy of pleasure, he was upholding the primacy of Aphrodite among the Olympians. He's gone further, however, and apparently made some rhetorical claim amounting to the *substitutability* of the concept and the Goddess. Socrates takes issue with this, and proceeds to gently scold Philebus. Socrates says that for his own part, he possesses an awe in respect to the names of the Gods that is supreme and, indeed, superhuman; accordingly, Socrates says, "*I* call Aphrodite by that name which is pleasing [*philon*] to her" (12c). These words could even perhaps be read simply as "that name which is hers."[134]

Similarly, later in the *Philebus* (30d) we read that "in the nature of Zeus a royal soul and a royal intellect emerges through the power of the cause"—i.e., causality, agency—"and in other deities other noble qualities, according to which each is called what pleases them [*philon ... legesthai*]." Here there is a chain

---

134 In accord with Homeric and other early poets' usage of *philon* (see LSJ, φίλος, I.2.c.).

formed by the Gods' agency or action, their emergent qualities, and the names or epithets they receive, which are at once "their own" and those which "please them". In the *Cratylus* (400d-e), similarly, Socrates states that it is evident that the names the Gods call *themselves* are true; while our own knowledge of them falls short of this absolute standard, nevertheless "there is a second kind of correctness, as is customary in prayers, that they be named whatever and from whencesoever pleases them [*chairousin*], and these we call them, since we know no other."[135]

Philebus trifles with the names of the Gods in a way that is, according to Socrates, all too human, presuming to replace Gods with *concepts*. Socrates is going to analyze the concept of pleasure; he does not intend to subject *Aphrodite* to such an analysis. We can compare again a passage from the *Cratylus*, immediately following the one I quoted above, where Socrates states categorically that in the inquiry which is to follow, he will inquire into the human contribution to the names of the Gods, that is, into the results of the human cognition resulting from theophany, and not into the nature of the Gods themselves (*Cratylus* 401a). This is not solely a question of piety. Rather, we can see from the explanation of the divine method later in the *Philebus* that Gods and concepts are clearly different *kinds of unit*. Persons of all kinds, we know, can hold together in the kind of unity *peculiar to a person as such* contradictions that would disintegrate a mere concept. And indeed, in the course of Socrates' and Protarchus' discussion about the nature of pleasure, it appears that *pleasures* are sufficiently heterogeneous as to pull apart the apparent integrity of the notion of Pleasure.

---

135 The ambiguity of naming in the *Cratylus* should be compared to the account of naming in the *Seventh Letter*, in which the name of a thing, together with its definition, image, and the knowledge of it, form a single holistic totality in the soul (*Epistle VII* 342c) which at once exhibits the thing itself but also presents itself in tension, even opposition to it. The name has its privilege over the other elements of this system inasmuch as it corresponds to the "true name" in denoting the object. This correspondence anchors the system by which a unique entity is joined to the totality of a language, but the "true name" remains ineffable, so to speak, simply on account of its irreducibility to this system.

And so, in the difference between Aphrodite and pleasure, we already have an illustration of the consequences of practicing the divine method, namely, we begin to discern different classes of unit, different kinds of 'one' with different kinds of integrity. When we consider the unity of a person, we know that certain sorts of manifest contradictions are consistent with their continued unity. Our friend changes in many ways, and may even have conflicting aspects enduring over time. Certain contradictions, however, would not be consistent with a *corporeal* person's unity insofar as they have a discrete position in space and time. If we were to consider our friend, however, through the lens of the doctrine of reincarnation, then we would find that all of these restrictions have been lifted. My friend may have been a different kind of animal at some time, or a human with completely different traits. This, I would argue, is why Plato is so interested in reincarnation: because if we accept the thought experiment, it reveals a very important kind of unity: a unit the same while any of its particular attributes vary—an individuality, thus, *beyond identity and difference*.

This procedure of investigating unities, testing them, figuring out how they hold together, is at once the inquiry into *the nature of unity itself or as such*, the question *What is unity?* We are always also pursuing this when investigating the mode of unity possessed by this or that unit. So this investigation goes right on up to the unit that is Unity as such, or 'the One Itself', *to hen auto*. The nature of *this* unit is investigated in what may be Plato's most important dialogue, the *Parmenides*. The investigation of the nature of unity in the *Parmenides* thus forms a crucial adjunct of the method outlined in the *Philebus*, and it also clearly gets us closest to what Plato could have meant by his statement that "the One is the Good", because more than any other dialogue, it tells us *what* unity is in itself, and no dialogue is similarly forthcoming about the Good. What is primarily said about the Good Itself is in the *Republic*, which states that it is "beyond being" or "beyond substance" (*epekeina tês ousias*), a characterization traditionally explicated with reference to the account of the One in the *Parmenides*, for reasons that will become evident.

The *Parmenides* tells of an encounter between the young Socrates and the two great philosophers and life-partners, Parmenides and Zeno of Elea in Italy, who have come to Athens to celebrate the Panathenaia. Socrates engages Zeno with regard to Zeno's famous paradoxes of plurality and motion, raising the notion of a theory of pure forms or ideas as a way of dealing with them. Such a theory is probably not to be attributed to Socrates alone, but seems to have been in the air, so to speak, especially in Pythagorean circles. The elderly Parmenides then proceeds to examine Socrates about the theory of ideas, showing a number of problems the theory faces, problems young Socrates is not quite ready to tackle. Parmenides acknowledges the necessity of *something* like the theory, though, simply so that we may orient ourselves in our discussions (what philosophers today call a heuristic device). But he says that it will be crucial to develop a rigorous dialectical procedure in connection with it. With regard to anything that one might take as an object of inquiry

> if you suppose that it is or is not, or that it experiences any other affection, you must consider what happens to it and to any other particular things you may choose, and to a greater number and to all in the same way; and you must consider other things in relation to themselves and to anything else you may choose in any instance, whether you suppose that the subject of your hypothesis exists or does not exist, if you are to train yourself to see the truth perfectly. (*Parm.* 136bc, trans. Fowler)

In a sense, Parmenides advances here a kind of coherentism, or even holism of meaning, that is, it seems that understanding anything requires placing it in relation to many other things, or possibly everything else. We see right away from this that Parmenides does *not* seem to hold the hypothesis that there is only one thing in the universe, the thesis of "numerical" or "existence monism" often attributed to him. There are many things in the universe and their relations to one another are both complex, and worth getting to know. Parmenides agrees to provide a demonstration of the sort of procedure he is recommending, and suggests that "I begin with myself, taking my own hypothesis and discussing the consequences of the supposition that the one exists or that it does not exist," (137b). Parmenides thus characterizes his hypothesis, not as that all things are one thing, but that "the One exists", that there is such a thing as *unity itself*.

I will not take up here the significance of this for our understanding of the extant fragments of Parmenides' own thought.[136] Rather, I will confine myself to the results of the discussion Parmenides proceeds to have with a boy even younger than Socrates, who happens to be named Aristotle—not, unfortunately, the philosopher of the same name. In this discussion, Parmenides first posits that the One Itself exists, and what the consequences are for it itself. This is naturally the part of the inquiry which concerns us most insofar as it speaks directly to the nature of 'the One'. Its result is that every property one tries to assert of the One Itself must be denied, because if the One is *also that*, then it is no longer One, no longer itself. The final result, in fact, is that the One Itself cannot even *be*, or be *one* (141e). This result provokes a certain incredulity, and so Parmenides makes a fresh start with his young interlocutor, and posits instead this time a One which is explicitly *a being*, with all that comes with that; and in this Second Hypothesis, as it is known, everything indeed comes in, because the One turns out to embrace every attribute that was previously denied it, *and* its negation. Neither in the First nor in the Second Hypothesis, then, is there room for the *One Itself* to be a singular item. In the First, the One Itself is nothing; in the Second, the One's own unity disintegrates in contradiction.

It becomes crucially important at this point to defend Plato from the charge of paradox mongering, because this is the implicit interpretation demanded by the monotheistic appropriation of Platonism. On a straightforward interpretation, nothing either in the First or the Second Hypothesis could answer to the monotheist notion of a singular God, either in its *transcendent* or in its *immanent* form, that is, it is neither a singular item beyond all things nor a singular item encompassing all

---

136 For an interpretation of the fragments of the historical Parmenides with which I am largely in agreement, though not necessarily with her reading of Plato, see Patricia Curd, *The Legacy of Parmenides: Eleatic Monism and Later Presocratic Thought* (Princeton: Princeton University Press, 1998).

things. But if the result of the entire procedure is nothing coherent, then the monotheist gets to proceed on the basis of what came to be known as "negative theology", a notion which, in fact, was born largely out of the necessity of dealing with this very problem. The "negative theology" interpretation of the *Parmenides* would have it that the One really must *be*, and be *one thing*, only, as Wittgenstein would say, in a very different context, "in a queer way". The negations and contradictions, on this interpretation, merely express our own inability to conceive the One Itself in its eminence. On this interpretation, we might say, the One is, and is one, *to the hilt*.

But another interpretation is possible, in which the One 'is' in a way much queerer indeed, but *also more rational*. For everything said with regard to the One in the First Hypothesis would be correct with respect to any individual conceived as *absolutely unique*. "But there isn't anything that's *absolutely* unique," someone will object. Indeed; and thus we proceed to the Second Hypothesis, where we see how un-individual and un-unique, any *one* that happens to be, must be, just insofar as *it is*. Neither side of this opposition can be eliminated. The hypothesis that there is such a thing as *unity itself* just yields these two poles of *austere* and *generous* unity, as Mary M. McCabe has termed it.[137]

A unit, therefore, is in one sense austerely one, and is just itself, in the most inalienable fashion, and is also, in the other sense, wide open onto all other things. This is the nature of unity. Now, where have we heard something like this before? In the description of the divine method in the *Philebus*, only there it was formulated differently, stating that every unit was *one*, and also *unlimited*, but most importantly, was some discrete multiplicity. It is this latter part which the investigation in the *Parmenides* into the nature of unity itself leaves open. Let's go back to the *Parmenides*, though, and consider a little further what we might make of the unity proposed in the First Hypothesis.

A truly 'austere' unit is utterly individual and unified, and hence utterly *peculiar*, that is, it is not comparable with anything else, for nothing about it can be considered separately from it, and potentially common with something else. Such a unit does not permit one to classify it. It is, of necessity, one of a kind, but

---

137 Mary Margaret McCabe, *Plato's Individuals* (Princeton: Princeton University Press, 1994), pp. 4-5.

one may not say that it has even this as a property, which would of course then render it *not one*. See, for instance, this passage from the First Hypothesis: after affirming that identity or sameness is "a nature separate from unity," Parmenides states that "if the One was to be affected by anything separate from unity, it would be affected so as to be more than one, and that is impossible," so "the One cannot be affected in the same way as another or as itself," and cannot thus be "like another or like itself" (*Parm.* 140a). No unit works *only* like this, to be sure. But the kind that functions most like this austere unit is the kind of unit with a *proper name*, the kind of unit, namely, that isn't a *what*, but a *who*.

Giving something a proper name is how we express its uniqueness, something we emphasize further by the categorical distinction we draw between 'what' and 'who'. If I ask *what something* is, I expect to be answered with a term that expresses its real or potential commonality with some number of other entities, whereas if I ask *who someone or somebody is*, I expect to be answered with something designating this entity *alone*. Now, anything I can ask the *who* question about, I can also ask the *what* question about. On the other hand, we don't generally ask the *who* question about just anything, but we recognize that one *could* give a proper name to a particular object of whatever sort.[138]

In this who-and-what, proper-name-and-common-noun practice, we see two fundamental aspects of anything's unity. In proper-name unity, we zero in immediately upon one unique entity, whereas in common-noun unity, we as it were fashion increasingly fine nets in which to catch a smaller and smaller number of entities, until we get down either to one, or to a set whose members are indiscernible according to the criteria of the 'net' we're using. We can't reduce the proper-name unity to the common-noun unity, or else we break it. A proper name *by definition* is not supposed to apply to more than one being. In practice, of course, things may have the same name, but that's

---

138 Although in ordinary language not all 'whats' are also 'whos', the capacity to universalize the 'who' function, and thus the mode of unity it represents, is essential to the *pantheistic* position. I would argue that this analysis shows that pantheism, just like monolatry and henotheism, is best understood on a polytheistic basis.

not how proper names work *in principle*. And even when we happen to arrive at a net that sorts a category down to a set with one member, we can't ensure that there couldn't be more than one being in the set unless we turn the sortal term (the 'net') in effect into a proper name, and then we've broken *that*.[139] We can name a lion 'Lion' and mean just this peculiar one we've met, but the two uses of 'lion' no longer function the same way from then on, and we show this in English by using the capital letter.

So we have two aspects of unity, one that designates unique unity, and the other that designates commonalities of some sort. In later Platonists like Iamblichus, Proclus and Damascius, there is a set of *prime units*, called 'henads'—a term that originates in the *Philebus*—who are unique, proper-named entities, namely the Gods themselves. These henads are 'in' the First Hypothesis of the *Parmenides* insofar as they are each a perfectly unique individual, while the *classifications* of them according to their properties yield the primary common terms for all of Being, which lies for its part in the Second Hypothesis.

We can see from the exchange near the beginning of the *Philebus* about Aphrodite that the distinction between proper names and common nouns was on Plato's mind, even if, like other advanced issues in Plato's thought, it was not discussed overtly or at length in the dialogues, but rather reserved for the private sessions of the Academy. And the issue of proper names is already in the *Philebus* linked to the consideration of the Gods, as well. If proper-named entities exhibit the primary modes of unity in primary fashion, what sort of entity best exhibits the formal properties of proper-naming? Certainly not ourselves, because so many kinds of *whatness* infuse our *whoness* as to overwhelm it, and to make our uniqueness, our proper-named unity, seem rather trivial by comparison. Indeed, it has been common enough, in the wake of the erasure of the very notion of a multiplicity of unique divine individuals, to attribute uniqueness as such purely to objects in space and time, or made out of some particular heap of stuff, or to things that can be uniquely designated conceptually, like the unique definition of a geometrical figure. To imagine a uniqueness *beyond* conceptual singularity, not inferior to it but superior, would in effect require

---

139 Something like this is at stake in the Stoic Chrysippus's paradox about identical twins 'Dion' and 'Theon'.

us to imagine something like the Gods, even if we didn't *believe* in such things. We would need to imagine individuals that could be both more peculiar, and more comprehensive, than mundane individuals can be. Such individuals would hold open the space of a *positive* or *existential difference* distinct from negative difference (*heterotês*).[140]

But if we conceive the Gods as unique in this way, how do we understand everything about them which they have in common: powers or potencies, including that of *being a God*, and relations with one another, some of which place them before or after one another in a pseudo-temporal sequence? These things can be taken so as to reduce the multiplicity of the Gods to some single unit. But it's not only on account of polytheistic piety that we don't do that ourselves, or shouldn't. As philosophers, we shouldn't do so because while that would make the Gods go away, it won't make *the problem of the nature of unity* go away. We would still have to recognize the metaphysical reality of the two different kinds of unity. Even if monotheism was all there had ever been, and all that any of us knew, this metaphysical problem would not go away, we just wouldn't have an example in the world driving us to work through it as polytheism does, so we would have to investigate it through thought-experiments. Indeed, without polytheism to spur philosophers on, the sensitivity to this problem languished significantly, even divorced from theological considerations, because it was so easy to treat what I have termed proper-name unity as only applying to entities *deficient* in common-noun unity, like spatio-temporal particulars that come and go all the time and can barely hold themselves together—which is why particulars conceived in this way feature prominently in the skeptical, unserious one-and-many problems Plato already complained about. Monotheists can think of their God as a proper-name unity, but as long as they want to make arguments for why there

---

140 Plato says in the *Sophist* (255e) that "each thing is different [*heteron*] from the rest not on account of its own nature, but through participating in the idea of the Different." 'Difference' here is not the source of individuation, but of *diacritical* or *differential identity*, what we might term *structural* identity, which is necessarily holistic and in that respect a unity subordinating the individual 'natures' that are distinguished *from one another* by it.

can be *only* one God based upon the *whatness*, the conceptual content attributed to this God, the distinction between proper-name unity and common-noun unity will be consistently and deliberately blurred by them.

Instead of dissolving the Gods into their common powers and relations, their common-noun unity, the Platonists, by contrast, developed complex accounts of the declination of these powers and relations from the metaphysically postulated uniqueness of each of these 'henads'. This satisfies the demands of piety, offering many solutions to practical problems that arise in polytheistic devotion, and also satisfies the demands of philosophy, by providing an account of how the second kind of unity (common-noun unity) *emerges* from the first kind of unity (proper-name unity).

So that's the trajectory of this doctrine in later antiquity; right now, we need to return to Plato himself and think about how the foundations of these ideas could have furnished him with the doctrine he presented in his lecture on the Good, and what that doctrine might have looked like. It is clear that Plato did *not*, in his lecture, discuss the Gods, at least not in a central way, or else it would certainly have been mentioned in the reports. Rather, he must have discussed how unity and the good operate generally, in all things. This probably took the form of a discussion about how, for each thing, its unity was its primary good. We know that a good deal of Plato's discussion concerned mathematics and astronomy, though, and we have not discussed these matters at all up to now. What would the role of mathematics and astronomy have been in Plato's talk?

With respect to astronomy, we know that in his dialogue the *Laws*, the importance of astronomy is that celestial motion is akin to "the motion and revolution and calculations of reason" (*Laws* 897c). Thus the role of astronomy in Plato's argument would have concerned the importance of a certain kind of motion in the cosmos, namely the kind that holds things together and fosters their orderly coexistence rather than their dispersion and disintegration, both individually and in harmonious conjunction. Plato would have sought to demonstrate thereby the way in which a single principle, the principle of unity, could govern all things in a just manner. Truly *universal* justice cannot, however, be such as to impose itself upon things as something separate from them. Hence we read in

Plato's *Timaeus* that "The best motion is that caused by itself in itself, for this is most akin to the motion of intelligence and of the All, while motion by another is worse," (89a).

Plato wishes to show that souls that are ordered in the right way individually will, just by virtue of that, also act collectively in the right way; and the best of souls, "which are good also with all virtue, we shall declare to be Gods, whether it be that they order the whole heaven by residing in bodies, as animals, or whatever the mode and method [...] Is there anyone who agrees with this view who will stand hearing it denied that 'all things are full of Gods'?" (*Laws* 899b).[141] We can see that Plato is not concerned to privilege the Gods of one realm over the others. Rather, once we have shown the key role played in the heavens by a motion *analogous to the motion of reason in the soul*, then we recognize that this kind of soul, wherever it exists, in whatever form, embodied or otherwise, is divine to whatever extent, and is giving order not only to itself but to the whole cosmos in its peculiar way, from *whatever* its station. Plato is quite explicit about the plurality of the divine force: "[A]s soul thus controls and indwells in all things everywhere that are moved, must we not necessarily affirm that it controls Heaven also?— Yes—One soul, is it, or more than one [*pleious*]? I will answer for you—'more than one'," (896e).

The 'motion' of soul which interests Plato is *circular* motion, because rectilinear motion is more complex than circular motion and inherently finite.[142] Circular motion is essentially of two kinds, one in which something rotates in place, centering itself, we might say, and the other, in which something revolves around something else, orienting itself to that;[143] and

---

141 Translations from the *Laws* are by R. G. Bury.

142 See the ten kinds of motion discussed at *Laws* 893b-894c. The formula for generating linear motion from the superimposition of circular motions was first clearly articulated by Nasir al-Din al-Tusi in the 13th c. CE (the 'Tusi couple'), though anticipated in remarks by Proclus in his commentary on Euclid (*In Eucl.* 106).

143 The two kinds of motion are described at *Timaeus* 40ab: the one, rotation, is "uniform motion in the same spot, whereby it conceives always identical thoughts about the same objects," the other, revolution, is "a forward motion due to its being

souls will engage in both kinds of motion, integrating themselves and orienting themselves to the best things other than themselves.

Clearly things aren't in general literally turning in circles around themselves and circling around other things, though some things, like the heavenly bodies, are, and hence the special interest in those things for the sake of the argument. This mechanical circular motion, however, is as it were a special case of a more general, *metaphysical* motion by which things are on the one hand centering the cosmos upon themselves, integrating it into themselves and giving internal order to themselves thereby, and at the same time recognizing the centrality of other things in other respects, and integrating themselves into the order of the totality 'outside'. These two 'motions' are inextricably entwined. I cannot successfully compose myself as a human without a sense of humanity as such, and the place of a mortal being such as myself in the universe, and what is incumbent upon me as a result. In a polycentric universe everything is in one respect a center for all things, while in other respects it is at the periphery, and this to varying degrees and in diverse ways. With this recognition, the notion of an *absolute* center becomes unnecessary, as Giordano Bruno, not without influence from the renewed acquaintance of the West with Platonic thought, would see and apply to astronomy almost 2,000 years later.

That these circular motions are metaphysical does not make them any less real. On the contrary, Plato presumably felt that he had to introduce astronomy into his lecture on the Good in order to integrate the elements of motion and time into his account of the nature of unity and the kinds of unity in things. Things existing in time bind themselves together, individually and severally, through *cycles*, something which of course has been recognized since the dawn of civilization in every tradition. That the circular motions are metaphysical, in other words, does not mean they are merely *metaphorical*. Rather, they are, so to speak, motions *of* motions, in the way that many disparate motions are oriented to a common end, the goal of some process; and so

---

dominated by the revolution of the Same and Similar" (trans. R. G. Bury), the latter phrase referring to the motion of Identity which together with that of Difference is constitutive of the Soul as such (*Tim.* 36c).

too, in a futher move of formalization, such goal-oriented motions are in principle cyclical, even if in fact they are only carried out one time, or even remain incomplete, because just insofar as they are ideal, they *could* repeat. So here again, we have our two notions of unity. Our discernment of that which is *formal* in something, what I have termed 'common-noun' unity here, can be understood as that in it which is *repeatable*, and thus involves the notion of cycles in time, of something returning to presence or returning to itself, as souls do, whether they are rational souls, which reflect upon their actions and their nature, or irrational souls, who return to or revolve upon themselves by doing the things necessary to repeat themselves and therefore sustain themselves as individuals in and through the difference brought about by time or as species, replicating themselves through the individuals here at this or that time.

The final component of Plato's lecture on the Good which I wish to analyze is the role of mathematics. What does mathematics mean for Plato, and why should the Good have so much to do with mathematics? To return to the *Philebus*, we find an important distinction between an arithmetic "of the people" and "of the philosophers" (*Phil.* 56d-e). In the former,

> arithmeticians reckon unequal units [*monadas*],
> for instance, two armies and two oxen and
> two very small or incomparably large units;
> whereas others [i.e., the 'philosophical'
> mathematicians] refuse to agree with them
> unless each of countless units is declared to
> differ not at all from each and every other
> unit.

A similar doctrine is suggested in the *Republic* (526a), which speaks of 'numbers' in which the One is such that "each unity [is] equal to every other without the slightest difference and admitting no division into parts,"[144] and Aristotle (*Metaphysics* 1080a) attributes to Platonists a doctrine of "incomparable" (*asymblêtos*) units alongside the conventional units of the mathematicians. Aristotle explains the nature of these units in this way:

---

144 Trans. Paul Shorey

if Two is first after One, and Three follows
Two, and so on with the other numbers, and
the units [*monades*] within each number are
comparable (for example the two units in the
first Two are comparable with each other, the
three units in the first Three are likewise
comparable, and so on with the rest of the
numbers), but the units of Two Itself are not
comparable with those of Three Itself, and
similarly for any two such numbers (and so
mathematical number is counted thus: one,
and then two, the latter resulting by the
addition of another unit to one, and three
results by the addition of another unit to two,
and similarly with the other numbers; but
these numbers are counted thus: One, and
then Two, the latter being composed of units
distinct from One, and then Three, without
including Two as a part, and so on with the
other numbers).[145]

If we widen our perspective beyond the narrow sense that
'number' has for us, we realize that such an "incomparable unit"
exhibits the mode of unity I characterized above as 'proper-
named'. For each of the attributes belonging to such a unit,
which are here termed 'monads',[146] are *peculiar* to that unit, and
not comparable to attributes in another, even in the case where
these attributes are as similar as the two monads in the number
Two and two of the three monads in the number Three. We see
the usefulness of the recourse to mathematics here, inasmuch as
it presents the case in the starkest terms possible. How much
more so, then, must the attributes of Aphrodite, for example, be

---

145 Trans. Hippocrates G. Apostle.
146 This is likely the first indication of the systematic distinction
later Platonists would draw between 'henads' and 'monads',
terms which seem synonymous in the *Philebus*, although the
discussion there is clearly less technical than the discussions
within the Academy it permits us to glimpse.

incomparable, in the Platonic view, with those of any other Goddess or God, be they ever so similar in our eyes?

When Aristotle discusses these matters, he is usually speaking about numbers in the sense we generally understand this term today, though not always. Hence, the discussion in *On the Soul* concerns the doctrine, held by Xenocrates, one of Plato's earliest successors at the Academy, that the soul is "a self-moving number" (*De Anima* 408b32). Here, clearly, something broader than mathematics as we know it is intended. We will better understand what is at stake in these discussions by broadening our sense of what is meant by the 'units' and 'numbers' in them.

For example, how are units that are not *comparable*, and thus do not *differ* from one another, in that sense at least, to be *distinguished* from one another? Such units, we read in Aristotle, can differ only in *position* (*thesis*) (*De Anima* 409a20) or in *order* (*taxis*) (*Categories* 5a30) or in *succession* (*ephexês*) (*Physics* 227a19-21, 29-31). This is clearly true of the natural number series, but it is *also* true of incomparable units in the sense of unique or peculiar existential individuals, namely that we must distinguish them by their relations to one another, since their attributes are peculiar to them. If we think of position, order, or succession in ways that might apply to *any* sort of entity, rather than mathematical or geometrical entities alone, we will see that this wider sense looks rather like the kinds of relations exhibited by elements in a *story* or a *picture*. Indeed, 'number', *arithmos*, always has in Greek a wider sense than the purely mathematical. To this we may compare the now-obsolete sense of numbering or calculation that was once included in English words for narration, such as 'tale' and 'tell', from the same root as German *Zahl*, "number".

The ultimate units, therefore, we may say, being unique in themselves, are distinguished by *iconic* and *narrative relations* with one another. And this is just the case with the Gods, for the Gods are not primarily understood by us as operating this or that *function*, which arises from comparison, but primarily as *incomparable units*, and we will tend to distinguish them, in addition to their proper names,[147] by referring to their familial

---

147 It is noteworthy that one of the maxims attributed to Pythagoras explicitly juxtaposes numbers and names: "What is the wisest thing? Number; but second, the one who put names

relations with other Gods in their pantheon, or the other relations they display in the myths and iconography peculiar to them. The science of these relations, both those internal to the divine individual as well as those external, is then the true 'theological arithmetic', and a rich field for future inquiry. The significance of Plato's remark that "the God eternally geometrizes",[148] therefore, is not to accord a naïve dignity to a science the limitations of which Plato is also well aware, but in the primary institution of *possible relations* and *spaces of relation* through the originary, mythic acts of the Gods, acts the meaning of which transcend categorization to inform all the sciences on a primordial level.[149]

As I remarked earlier, it is very unlikely that Plato explicitly spoke of the Gods in his lecture on the Good. In a certain respect, this is because he didn't *need* to. All around him temples hummed with the daily life of devotion, temples to the Gods of many nations. The noise and colors and smells of festivals were always in the air. That all of this could go away was inconceivable, even nonsensical. It is *we* who need to approach Plato's thought from an explicitly polytheistic perspective, and by 'we' I by no means intend merely *we polytheists*, but *we moderns* generally. For whatever our intellectual project, it will run aground if the notion of the *Idea* remains trapped in the deadlock of form and matter, the legacy of the distortion consequent upon the monotheistic construct of a Platonism without the Gods.

In authentic Platonism, Ideas were always inseparable from the lives of souls, mortal souls like ours, but most importantly the immortal souls of the Gods, who do not suffer from our deficiencies. I have had little occasion to speak of Ideas in this essay, which would seem surprising under the conventional

---

to things," (Diels-Kranz 58c4, quoted by Iamblichus, *Vita Pythagorae* 82).

148 As reported by Plutarch, *Quaes. Conv.* 8.2.1.

149 On this primary collective activity of the Gods, see in particular "The Second Intelligible Triad and the Intelligible-Intellective Gods," *Méthexis* 23 (2010), pp. 137-157. [Reprinted in *Essays on the Metaphysics of Polytheism in Proclus* (New York City: Phaidra Editions, 2014).]

impression of Platonism as fundamentally concerned with these entities. In this, however, I merely follow Plato himself, who explains that as the Sun is to the things of the world, principle both of their very being and of their visibility, so is the Good to the Ideas, that by which they are and are known (*Republic* 509b). But the Good is the Unity of each thing, and so the study of the modes of unity enfolds and takes up into itself the inquiry into forms or ideas. The ultimate mode of unity, in turn, is the peculiar or unique; and the most unique of things are the Gods themselves. For the Platonist, this is how the priority of the Gods in and beyond the cosmos offers itself to our understanding.

ABOUT THE AUTHOR

Edward P. Butler received his PhD in Philosophy from the
New School for Social Research in 2004 for his
dissertation "The Metaphysics of Polytheism in Proclus".
He has published regularly in academic journals, edited
volumes and devotional anthologies, as well as serving on
the editorial board of the independent academic journal
Walking the Worlds: A Biannual Journal of Polytheism and
Spiritwork, and writing a column, Noēseis, for
Polytheist.com. His work focuses primarily on Platonism,
on the polytheistic philosophy of religion, and on
mythological hermeneutics, with additional focus on
Egyptian, Hellenic and Hindu theologies and philosophies.
Many of his publications are available free from his
website, Henadology: Philosophy and Theology, which
also features his online Theological Encyclopedia of the
Goddesses and Gods of the Ancient Egyptians. In
addition he is active on Twitter @EPButler.

Made in the USA
San Bernardino, CA
23 February 2019